WARMING

57 Pre-Session

UP THE

Training

CROWD!

Activities

WARMING

57 Pre-Session

UP THE

Training

CROWD!

Activities

Dave Arch • Rich Meiss

Introduction by Bob Pike, CSP

Jossey-Bass
Pfeiffer

Creative Training Techniques
Press

Copyright © 2000 by Jossey-Bass/Pfeiffer and Creative Training Techniques Press

Library of Congress Cataloging-in-Publication Data

Arch, Dave.
    Warming up the crowd! : 57 pre-session training activities / Dave
Arch, Rich Meiss.
      p. cm.
    ISBN 0-7879-5141-2
    1. Employees—Training of—Methodology.   2. Oral communication.
    3. Visualization.   I. Meiss, Rich.   II. Title.
    HF5549.5.T7M4225   2000
    658.3'124—dc21   99-42893

Printed in the United States of America

Published by

Jossey-Bass Pfeiffer

350 Sansome Street, 5th Floor
San Francisco, California 94104-1342
(415) 433-1740; Fax (415) 433-0499
(800) 274-4434; Fax (800) 569-0443

Creative Training Techniques Press

7620 West 78th Street
Minneapolis, MN 55439
(800) 383-9210
(612) 829-1954; Fax (612) 829-0260

Visit our website at: www.pfeiffer.com

Visit our website at:
www.creativetrainingtech.com

Acquiring Editor: Matthew Holt
Director of Development: Kathleen Dolan Davies
Senior Production Editor: Dawn Kilgore
Manufacturing Supervisor: Becky Carreño
Cover Design: Brenda Duke

Printing 10 9 8 7 6 5 4 3 2 1

This book is printed on acid-free, recycled stock that meets or exceeds the minimum GPO and EPA requirements for recycled paper.

Contents

1. Brainteasers   1

Introduction

"Warming Up the Crowd!"

When two of our Senior Training Consultants, Dave Arch and Rich Meiss, told me of the title for their new book, all I could think was, "What a great name for a book!" And then shortly on the heels of that thought came, "The need for this book is enormous!"

In all probability your company's training budget does not allow the luxury of a "warmup act" for your training session. No one comes and tells a few jokes and schmoozes with the crowd prior to introducing you. Don't feel bad. No one supplies such an act for me either. However, in spite of this fact, I try never to make the mistake of underestimating the importance of using a warmup activity in all of my training sessions.

The value of a pre-session activity has been proven again and again:

- Those participants who get to class early have something immediately to do that will help them break their preoccupation and get focused on that which is to come.

- When used immediately following a break, each of these activities rewards those participants who are back on time—giving them a value-added piece.

- Networking happens quite automatically as participants interact with participants in a natural and unforced manner—seeking to compare notes on their approaches to the activity.

- The trainer has a natural opener as she or he can begin by asking the participants how they are progressing on the pre-session activity.

- Consequently, momentum has been generated prior to the "official" beginning of the session—creating an energized atmosphere right from the onset of the training.

If you've trained for longer than a week, you know how important that last benefit can be—never having to begin your training from a "dead stop."

Within the covers of this book, you will find one proven pre-session activity after another. I believe that many will find their way into your own training repertoire, just as they have into mine.

Bob Pike, CSP, CPAE
Chairman/CEO and Founder
Creative Training Techniques International

Editor and Founder
Creative Training Techniques Newsletter

Preface

One of the keys to good training is to get participants ready to learn before you start presenting content. Because we typically have so much content to cover in today's information-packed world, we start delivering content immediately. Consider the following alternative: you must go slow before you can go fast. What I mean by that is we need to get the participant ready to learn. Perhaps this example will be helpful:

> I grew up on a farm in western Minnesota. I always enjoyed the spring of the year, because it meant that we would get to plant the seeds and see the results of our work begin to sprout forth. But before we planted the seeds, we spent a good deal of time preparing the soil—getting it ready to accept the seed. The farmer knows that to get the best harvest, he must first prepare the soil.

Good trainers know the same thing. To get the best results from the training seeds about to be planted, the "soil of the mind" must first be prepared. This is the reason that we at Creative Training Techniques believe so strongly in the value of a good opening for our training sessions. Even before the formal opening of the session, there is often valuable time to prepare the learner. That is the purpose of the exercises in this book—"to capture the learner before the training begins."

Dave and I designed this book to be a ready-to-use resource of exciting, proven warmup activities you can use immediately. Each activity is designed so that you can easily reproduce it for your participants, either in hard copy or, in some cases, as a transparency. Accompanying each warmup is a page that gives you the solution, and also gives you preparation tips and application ideas.

Many of these exercises can be used in other ways as well. Some would be a good energizer to give participants a lift. Others would be useful as exercises to teach content or ways to review content. Where appropriate, we have made some of those suggestions in the "Application" portion of the exercise.

Coauthor and fellow CTT trainer Dave Arch and I would enjoy hearing other application ideas or enhancements to any of these warmups. Please send them to us at:

Creative Training Techniques International
7620 West 78th Street
Minneapolis, MN 55439

Maximize the results of your training by getting your participants in the learning mood before your session begins. Both the trainers and the session participants will benefit from doing so.

Here's wishing you good training.

Rich Meiss
Minneapolis, Minnesota
September 1999

About the Authors

Dave Arch, best-selling author and nationally acclaimed training conference speaker, has written seven resource books for the training industry, including the "Tricks for Trainers" books and videos, in addition to his popular monthly column in the *Creative Training Techniques Newsletter*.

Drawing upon twenty-five years of training experience, Dave travels for Creative Training Techniques, customizing and presenting four different participant-centered "train the trainer" seminars and keynotes, including the cutting-edge seminar entitled "Creative Training Techniques for Distance Learning."

Dave's clients include the Nabisco Company, US West Communications, the U.S. Postal Service, the Internal Revenue Service, Kimberly-Clark, the National Education Association, the Canadian Postal Service, Napa Auto Parts, and the U.S. Central Intelligence Agency.

Rich Meiss has played a key role in the human resources industry since 1972, holding executive positions with Personal Dynamics Institute, Carlson Learning Company, and Creative Training Techniques International, Inc. He is currently executive director of the Meiss Education Institute.

He has personally worked with over 10,000 trainers in promoting, marketing, and delivering effective training programs. He has conducted workshops and seminars in more than 150 cities in the United States, Canada, Mexico, Europe, and Asia.

An inspiring speaker, Rich delivers keynote addresses each year to businesses, organizations, and trade associations. His topics vary, but his theme always centers around increasing personal and organizational productivity through developing the "human side" of enterprise. Rich is an active member of the National Speakers Association and the American Society for Training and Development, and he has addressed his peers at national conferences.

Rich's clients have ranged from small to large businesses, government, education, and health care groups. They include BMW, Southwestern Bell Telephone, Essex Corporation, Northland Insurance, Rafferty's Restaurants, the U.S. Food and Drug Administration, Minnesota Department of Transportation, and Baxter Healthcare.

Rich has coauthored training programs with Bob Pike, Dr. Denis Waitley, and Dr. Michael O'Connor, and he has published numerous articles in trade journals. Special recognitions include being listed in "Who's Who in the Midwest" and "Emerging Leaders in America."

Rich is also the president of the Center for Personal Responsibility, a nonprofit organization dedicated to "balancing personal rights with personal responsibility."

WARMING UP THE CROWD!

57 Pre-Session

Training

Activities

This book is dedicated to the tens of thousands of
trainers and educators we have trained in the past
and will train in the future—may you find
just the right warmup exercises in these pages.

Special thanks to Bob Pike
and the Creative Training Techniques trainers
for their creativity and support in developing this book.

Dave Arch and Rich Meiss

Brainteasers

Three women are all
wearing swimming suits.
Two are smiling
but they're sad.
One is crying but she's happy.
Who are they?

Hint: These women aren't going near the water.

Beauty Brainbuster

Preparation

Copy the opposite page onto a transparency and get ready to have some fun with your participants as they attempt to solve the riddle.

Solution

The women are competitors in a beauty pageant.

Application

Discuss as a group what makes the solution to this brainteaser so difficult. You'll find that a lot of it has to do with our assumptions—carrying us in a direction that doesn't help solve the problem at all.

That's true with all problem solving situations! We must learn to neutralize our assumptions (or at least recognize them) before we may move successfully toward solving any problem that faces us at work or in our personal lives.

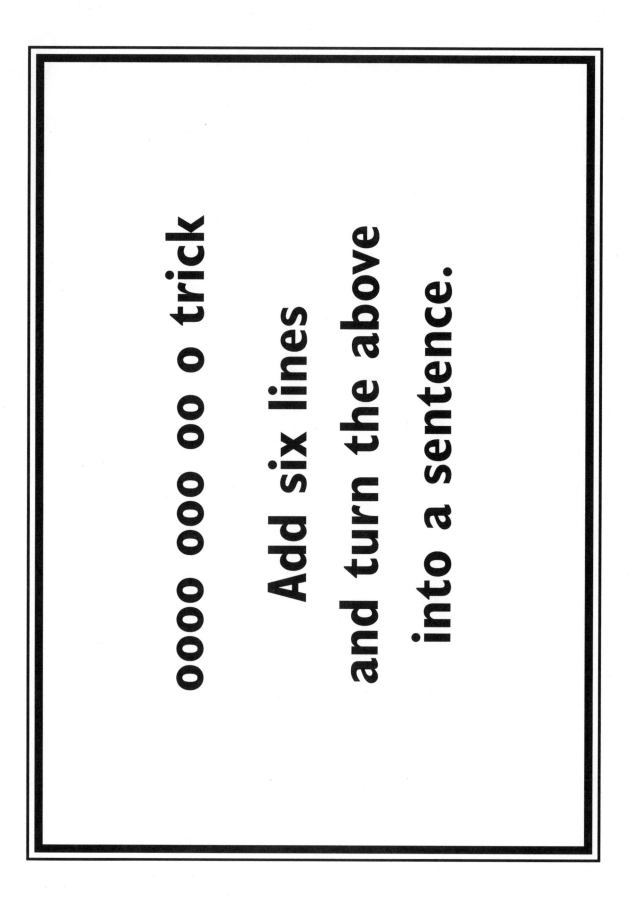

oooo ooo oo o trick

Add six lines
and turn the above
into a sentence.

Between the Lines

Preparation

Make a transparency from the master on the opposite page and you'll have a great pre-session activity to really warm up the crowd in your next training session.

Solution

By adding lines in the appropriate places, you'll have the phrase "Good dog do a trick."

Application

Details are important. Simple (and small) lines make a meaningless design into a sentence that communicates.

We need to watch the details in all that we do if we are to maintain quality in our work.

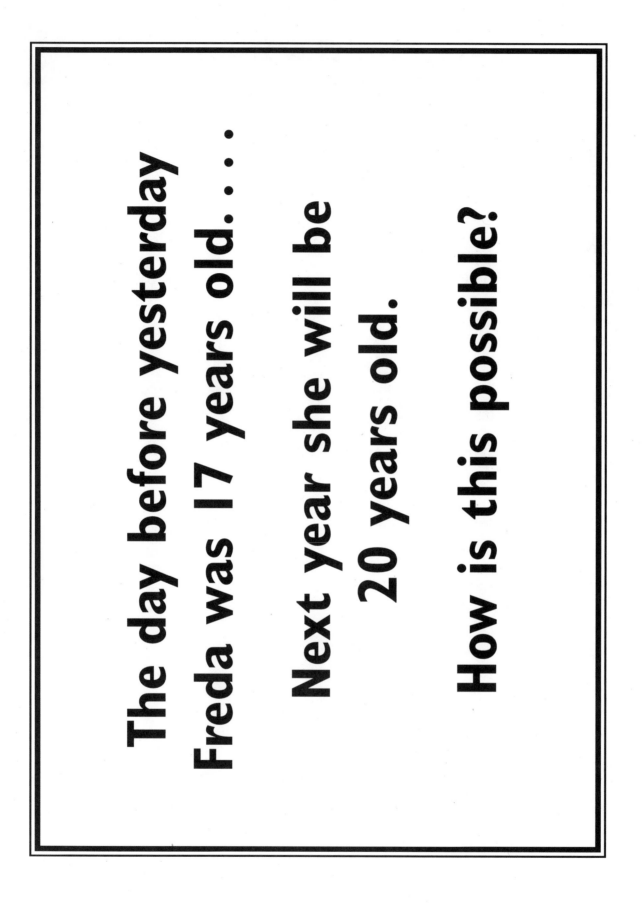

The day before yesterday Freda was 17 years old. . . .

Next year she will be 20 years old.

How is this possible?

Birthday Baffler 1

Preparation

Copy the opposite page onto a transparency and use it to create energy in your training room. To maximize the energy, award a prize to the first person who solves the puzzle.

Solution

Freda's birthday is December 31. This statement was spoken on January 1.

Application

The question on the transparency is very important! Rather than using the word "impossible" when we hear of a situation or a desired result, we need to ask, "How is this possible?" Such a question always opens our minds to seek possible solutions, just as it did in this situation.

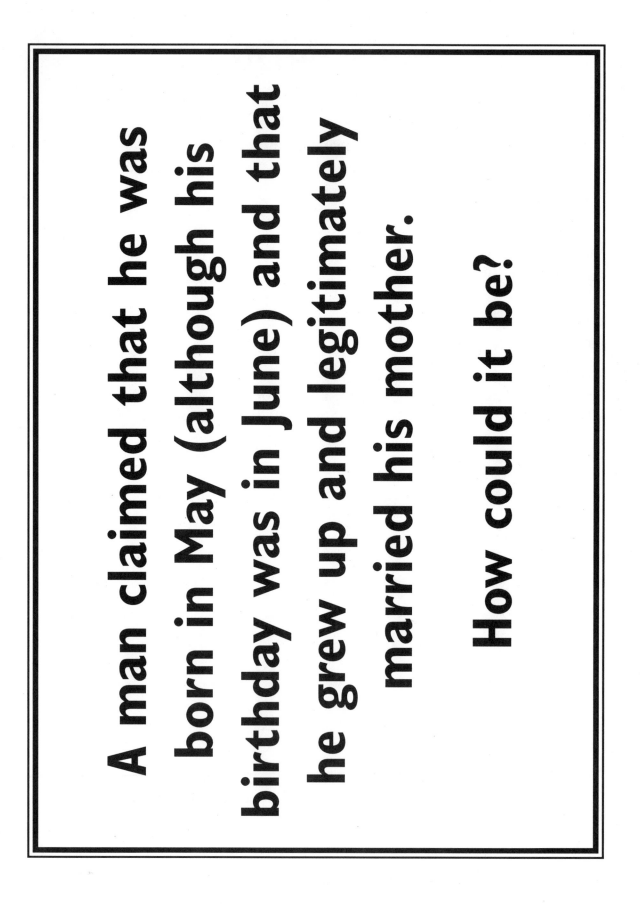

A man claimed that he was born in May (although his birthday was in June) and that he grew up and legitimately married his mother.

How could it be?

Birthday Baffler 2

Preparation

Duplicate the overhead master on the opposite page and use it as a great way to jump-start your training session when your participants are coming back from a break.

Solution

The man was born in the city of May in the month of June, and he grew up to become a judge who performed the wedding ceremony of his widowed mother and her second husband.

Application

Paradigm shifts are easily demonstrated with this brainteaser as words and their meanings change as our paradigm shifts. This is a great brainteaser for any communication subject!

What does the following mean?

RESAET NIAR
BNWORU OYE
KAMN ACUOY

Build Your Own Brainteaser

Preparation

Build your own brainteaser using the pattern on the opposite page.

1. Decide upon a content-based phrase that you'd like your participants to try to decipher.

2. Print the phrase backward onto a transparency.

3. Divide the letters into erroneous words.

Solution

Using the above steps in reverse, the phrase on the opposite page reads: "YOU CAN MAKE YOUR OWN BRAINTEASER"

Application

This works great anytime you need a brainteaser that's very content-specific! Don't be afraid to set a time limit or give prizes to the table team that deciphers the phrase first. It will only add to the excitement!

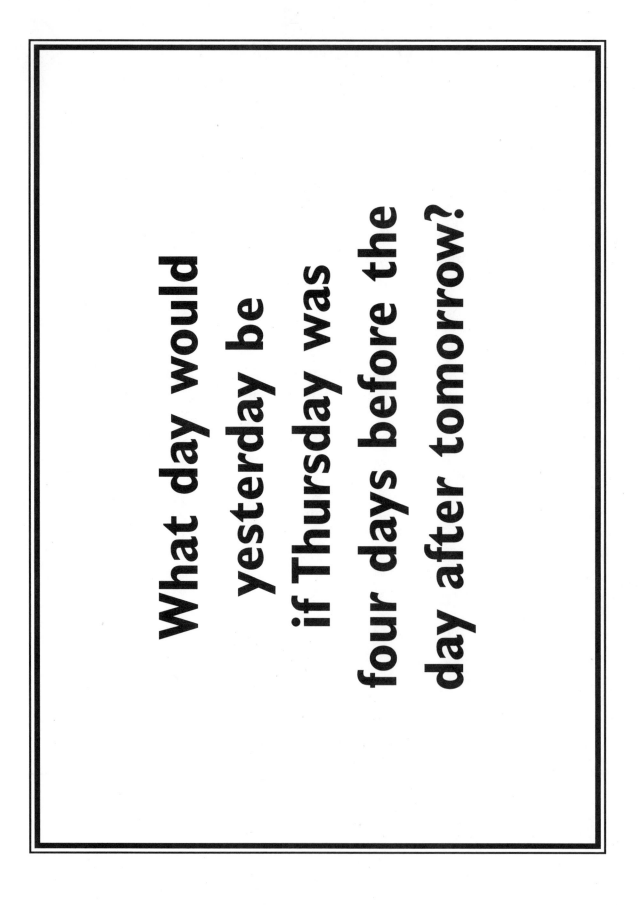

What day would yesterday be if Thursday was four days before the day after tomorrow?

Calendar Craziness

Preparation

Copy the opposite page onto a transparency and have it on the overhead screen about three minutes before you're actually ready to start. You'll be amazed at how well such an activity helps you start immediately with energy.

Solution

Friday

Application

Pose the question, "What process did you go through to solve the puzzle?" This question will lead you to the definition of a process that is helpful in all problem solving situations.

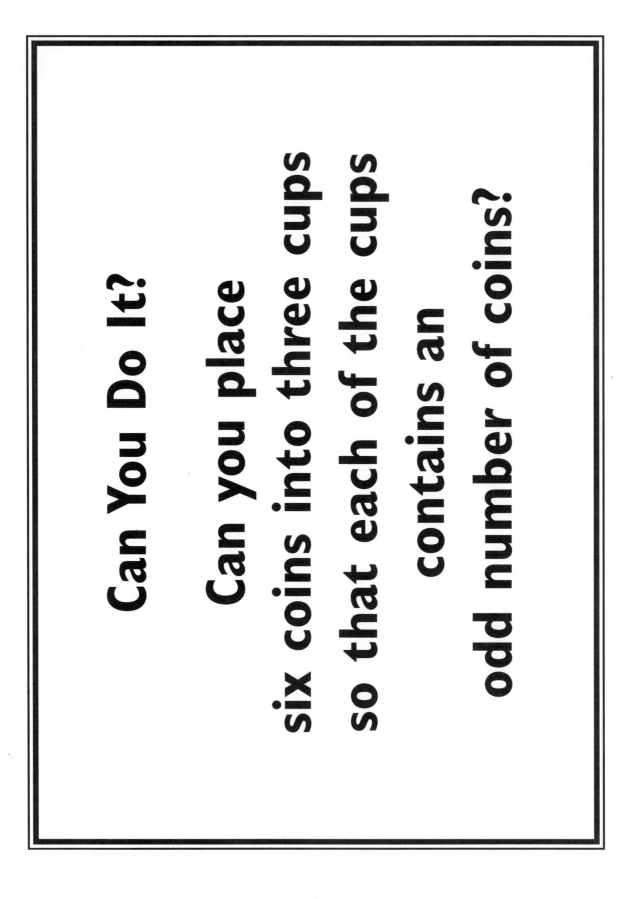

Can You Do It?

Can you place
six coins into three cups
so that each of the cups
contains an
odd number of coins?

Coin Cups

Preparation

On each table in the training session, place three paper cups and six pennies. Do not have the cups stacked on the table. Instead, have the three cups separated with two pennies in each cup. Copy the opposite page onto a transparency to introduce this challenge to your group.

Solution

One solution is to place three pennies into one cup. Then place two pennies into another cup. Stack an empty cup inside of the cup with two pennies and place one penny into this inside cup. You will have fulfilled the challenge.

Application

There is more than one solution to this problem. Consequently, it's a great brainteaser to prompt a discussion about how often, in our search for the "right answer," we can miss the best answer.

Don't be afraid of multiple good ideas. Keep looking!

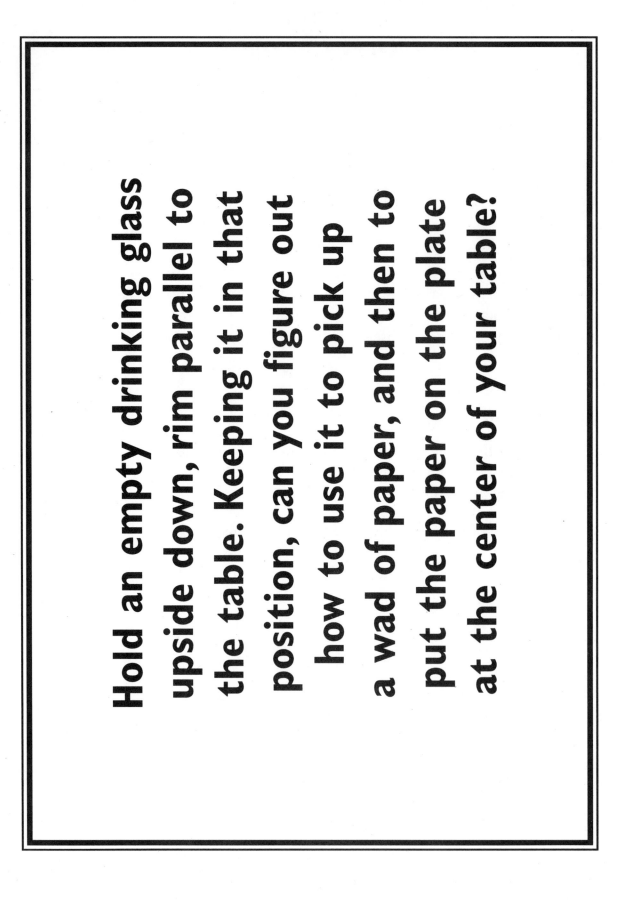

Hold an empty drinking glass upside down, rim parallel to the table. Keeping it in that position, can you figure out how to use it to pick up a wad of paper, and then to put the paper on the plate at the center of your table?

Creative Lifting

Preparation

Copy the opposite page onto a transparency and display it on your overhead. On each table have a plate at the center of the table, and a glass and small wad of paper about the size of a ping-pong ball (or slightly smaller depending on the glass size) at each place.

Solution

Place the upside-down glass over the wad of paper and start spinning the glass centrifugally, to get the wad of paper circling around the inside of the glass. Lift the glass while spinning, and when you have it over the plate stop spinning—the wad of paper falls onto the plate!

Application

Creativity is always needed when a seemingly impossible situation presents itself. However, creativity is often a matter of trial and error.

We must be willing to risk failure to find success.

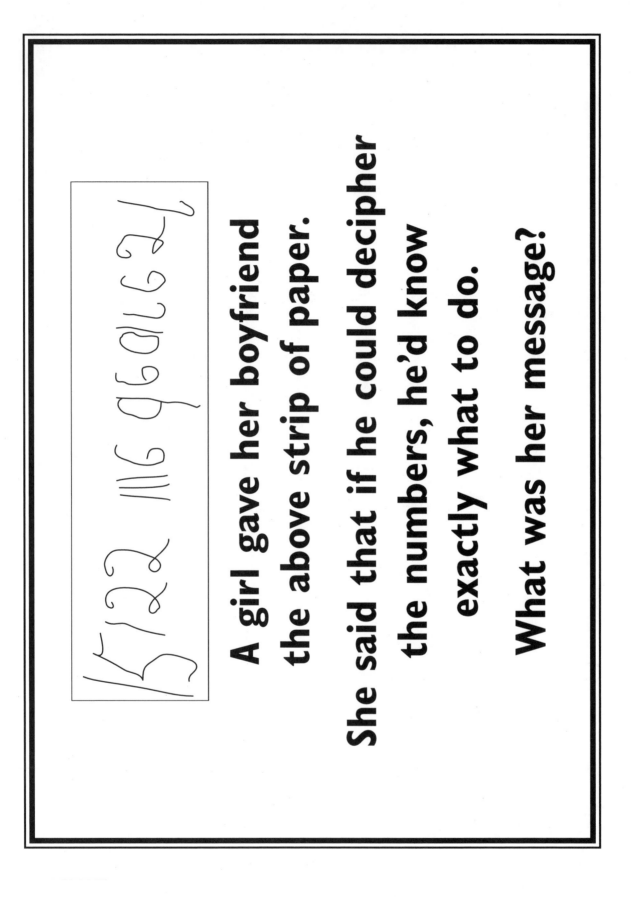

A girl gave her boyfriend the above strip of paper.

She said that if he could decipher the numbers, he'd know exactly what to do.

What was her message?

Delightful Digits

Preparation

Copy the master on the opposite page onto a transparency for use on the overhead. Distribute a regular white photocopy of the opposite page to each participant in your class.

Solution

If you turn the paper over and then upside down, holding it up to the light you will see that the cryptic message actually reads, "Kiss Me Dearest.".

Application

We cannot expect different results if we continue to keep doing things the same way!

We have been taught a certain way to read a message, but that approach won't work in this situation. Willingness to try new things often yields exciting discoveries.

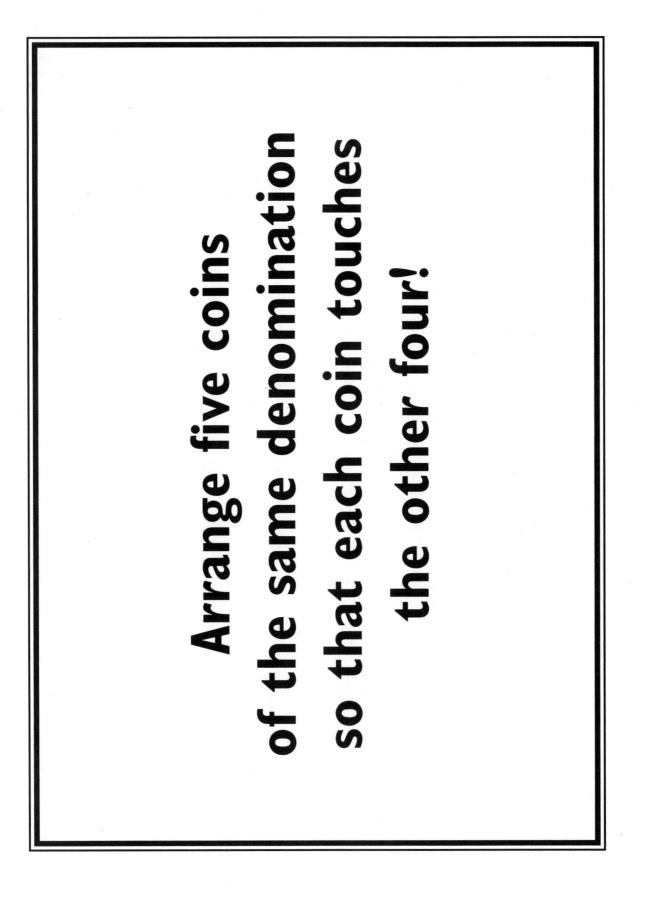

Arrange five coins of the same denomination so that each coin touches the other four!

Five-Coin Touch

Preparation

Copy the opposite page onto a transparency for use on your overhead. To use this brainteaser with your class, provide five coins of the same denomination on each table. Try making this a team exercise—it helps raise the energy level in the room.

Solution

Place one coin on the table, with two coins lying on top of it, touching at their two inside edges. Then put the last two coins—touching tepee fashion—resting on the bottom-most coin and touching the other two coins as a natural result of their leaning toward each other. *Hint:* You must hold onto the coins for this activity to work.

Application

Persistence is vital to problem solving, which this brainteaser helps to underscore. How many failures do your participants have before their success?

What can we do to get ourselves and our company more comfortable with the process of finding success?

Can you erase
one letter at a time
from the word below
and leave a completely
new word each time?

SNOWING

Letter Elimination 1

Preparation

Copy the opposite page onto a transparency and use this one in conjunction with Letter Elimination #2, which follows. You might use one with the entire group, and then turn the table teams loose to work on the second one. Or you might even have one of the letter eliminations done by each participant and then the other with the entire group working together. There are some good teamwork applications in this brainteaser!

Solution

snowing, sowing, swing, wing, win, in, i

Application

If you choose to do one of the letter eliminations as an entire group and the other in table teams, you might follow up with a discussion about whether it was easier to solve the puzzle in the big group or the smaller group, and why. Such a discussion would lead to interesting discoveries about what types of projects are done best by individuals, in a small group, or in a large group.

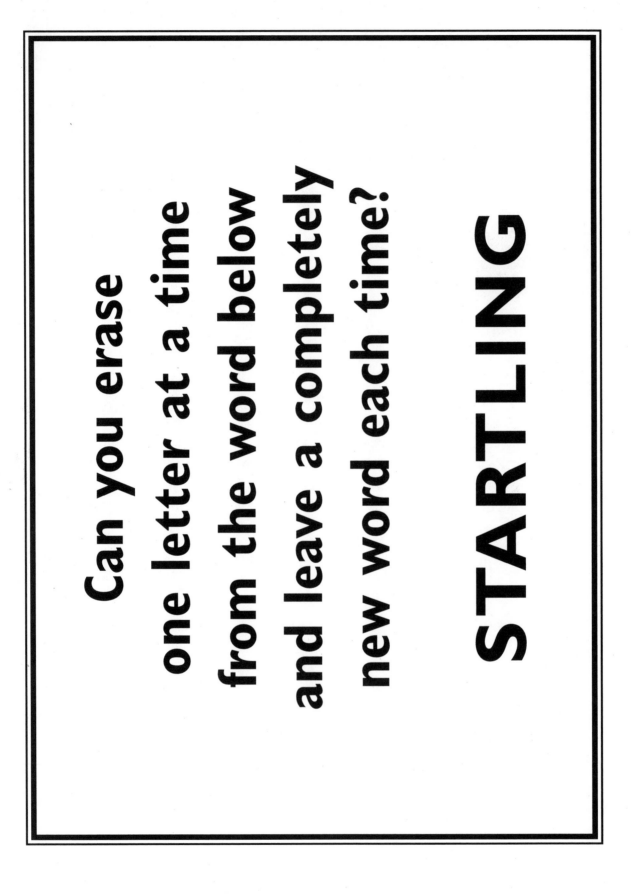

Can you erase one letter at a time from the word below and leave a completely new word each time?

STARTLING

Letter Elimination 2

Preparation

Duplicate the opposite page onto a transparency for use in presenting this puzzle to the class. As an impromptu exercise, simply print the word on a flip-chart page and have the group try their hand at it.

Solution

startling, starling, staring, string, sting, sing, sin, in, i

Application

Picasso said, "Every act of creation is first of all an act of destruction." Every time something new is created, something else was destroyed. This puzzle illustrates that fact as a new word is created by the "destruction" of the previous word. Likewise, in order to move forward, often we must leave behind friends and familiar routines.

This is a great puzzle for getting people ready to embrace change in any organization.

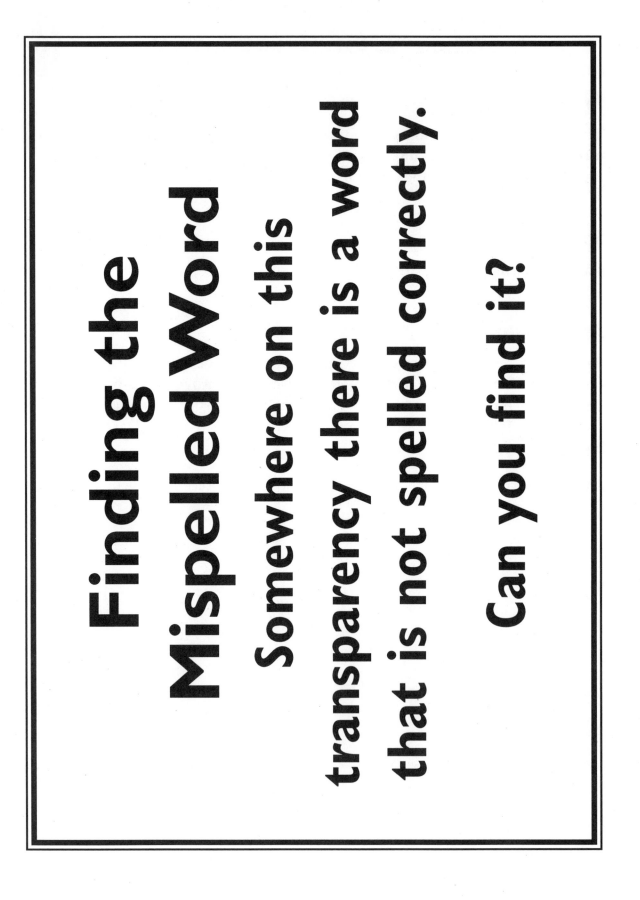

Finding the Mispelled Word

Somewhere on this transparency there is a word that is not spelled correctly.

Can you find it?

Proofreading: Finding the Misspelled Word

Preparation

Duplicate the opposite page onto a transparency for introducing the brainteaser to your group.

Solution

The word "mispelled" is misspelled.

Application

Thinking "outside of the box" is crucial in any process of evaluation. More often than not, participants do not consider the title of the transparency as part of the puzzle. However, the instructions do make it clear that the entire transparency is the field of focus. When looking for the solution to a problem, consider the *entire* situation.

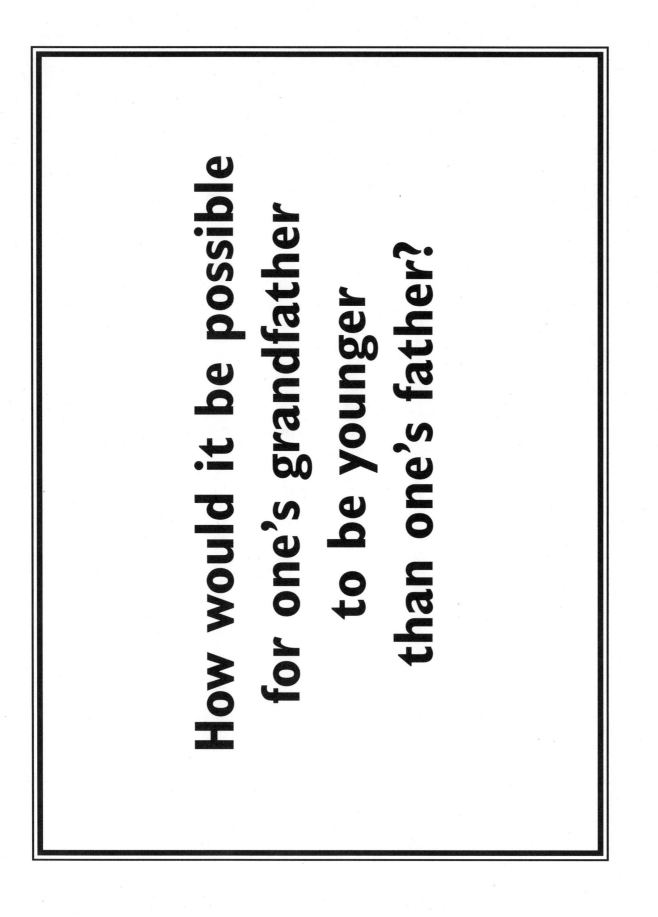

How would it be possible for one's grandfather to be younger than one's father?

Relationally Speaking 1

Preparation

Copy the opposite page onto a transparency for use in introducing this puzzler to your participants.

Solution

One's maternal grandfather could easily be younger than one's own father.

Application

Rather than debating whether or not something is possible, it is much better to begin with the question, "How would it be possible . . . ?" That's a great attitude to have in any training session! Why not use this puzzle to help generate that perspective in your next class?

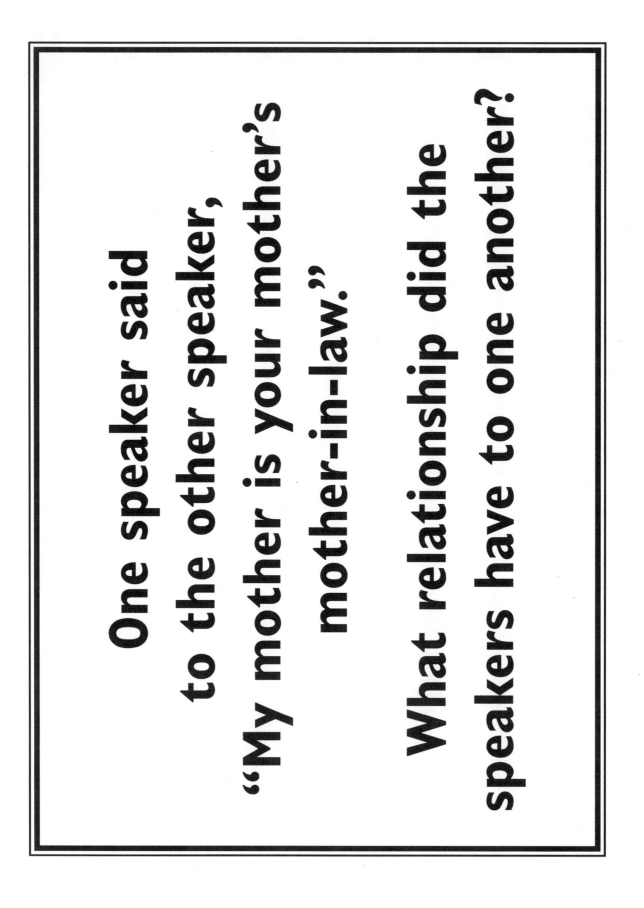

One speaker said to the other speaker, "My mother is your mother's mother-in-law."

What relationship did the speakers have to one another?

Relationally Speaking 2

Preparation

Duplicate the opposite page onto a transparency for creating energy in a room when people are returning from break or lunch.

Solution

The relationship could either be father and child or paternal uncle/aunt and nephew/niece.

Application

This is a great brainteaser anytime you're trying to emphasize the relationship between one aspect of the business and another (customer service/ profit; quality/customer satisfaction; cost control/profit, and such).

The relationships between business components are not always easy to recognize, but they are always important.

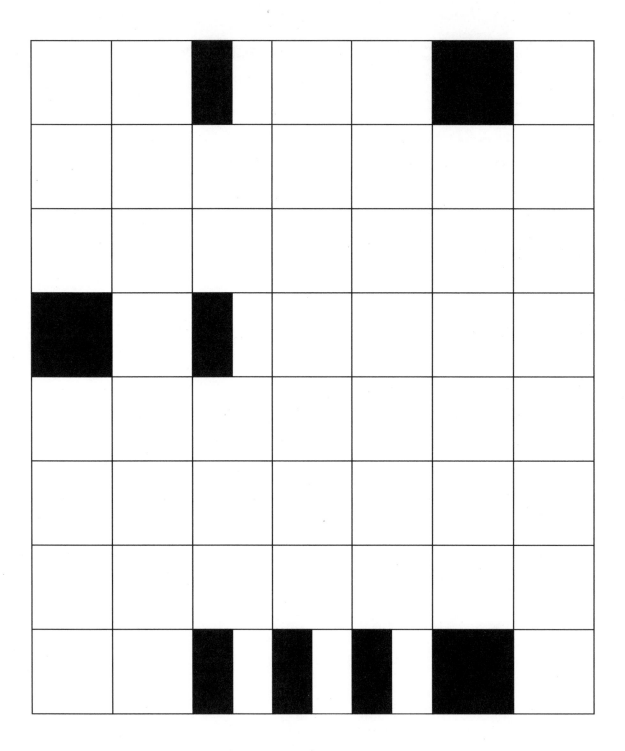

Secret Message

Preparation

Copy the opposite page onto a transparency and also duplicate it so that each person in your class gets a copy. Ask them to decipher the message.

Solution

The word is "HELLO." You can see it by holding the page flat and looking across the page from the bottom to the top. Closing one eye also helps you see the message.

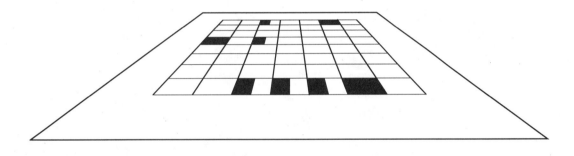

Application

We often need to view a situation from a fresh perspective in order to see it more clearly. Breaking some rules (as in this example, the rules for reading) is also often a necessary component to solving a problem.

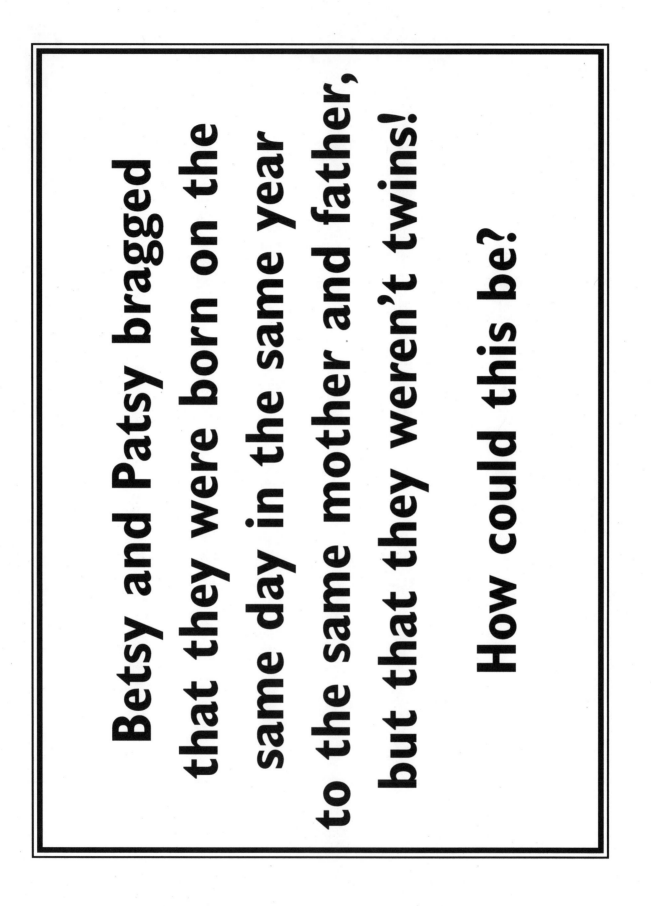

Betsy and Patsy bragged that they were born on the same day in the same year to the same mother and father, but that they weren't twins!

How could this be?

Tricky Twins

Preparation

Copy the opposite page onto a transparency for introducing this brain-teaser to your participants.

Solution

They were two sisters of triplets!

Application

Typically, participants overcomplicate this one. When they hear the solution, they groan. "What causes us to overcomplicate this brainteaser?" is a great question to begin analyzing why we tend to overcomplicate many situations we face.

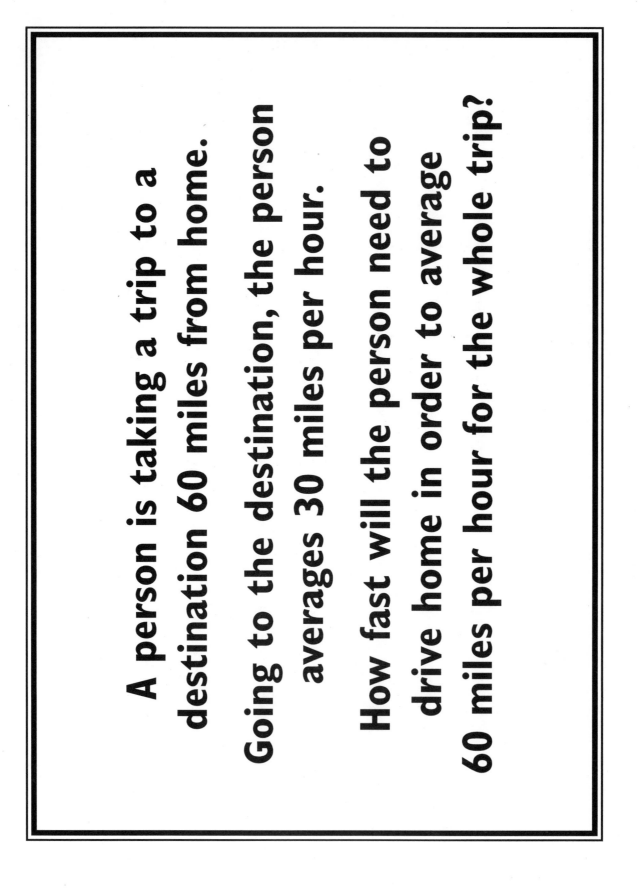

A person is taking a trip to a destination 60 miles from home.

Going to the destination, the person averages 30 miles per hour.

How fast will the person need to drive home in order to average 60 miles per hour for the whole trip?

Tripping!

Preparation

Copy the opposite page onto a transparency, and you'll find yourself with a brainteaser particularly suited to those participants with analytical (mathematical) minds.

Solution

It will be impossible to average 60 miles per hour for the whole trip because the driver used the necessary two hours on the first leg of the trip. If the driver had used only 1 hour and 59 minutes, it would be possible theoretically (traveling at nearly the speed of light) to return in one minute. However, because the driver consumed the entire two hours, this has now become an impossibility.

Application

Just as there are some things in life that seem impossible but in fact are possible, likewise there are some things in life that seem possible but truly are impossible. It's a difficult, but necessary, reality to face both in business and in our personal lives. This is one of the few brainteasers that illustrates that fact very well.

Circle Cards

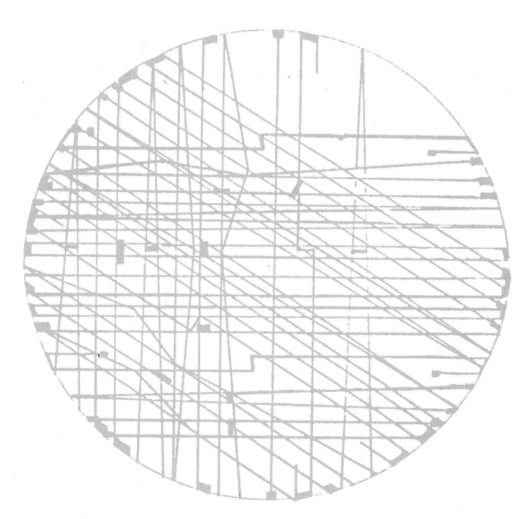

Look across the circle.

What does it say?

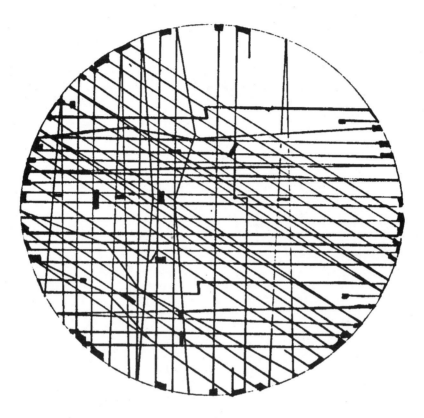

Leadership

Preparation

Make copies of the master sheet on the opposite page.

Solution

A Leader Is A

Person Who

Has Followers

Application

Look at leadership in a new way. You can't appoint leaders—people must choose to follow them. Are we doing all we can around our organization to help develop leadership skills so that our people choose to follow us?

Look across the circle.
What does it say?

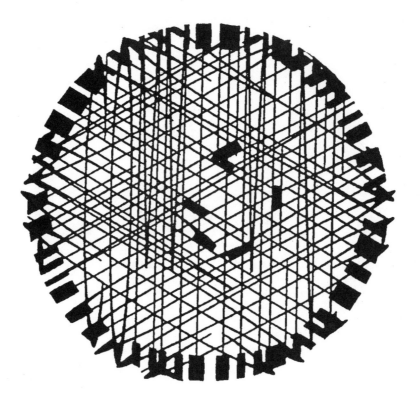

Change Management

Preparation

Make copies of the master sheet on the opposite page.

Solution

Commitment

Competency

Coordination

Application

To really make changes work in an organization, there are three key ingredients:

- We all need to be committed to the new change.
- Each person needs to be competent with his or her contribution.
- There must be a coordinated effort to make it all work.

The three keys to effective change are commitment, competency, and coordination.

Look across the circle.

What does it say?

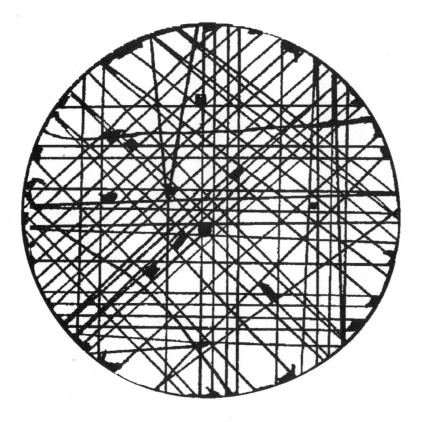

Technophobia

Preparation

Make a handout from the master on the opposite page.

Solution

If you can

use an ATM,

You can use

A computer.

Application

Sometimes, people need to look at things differently to see all that there is to see. This is especially true in overcoming the fear of technology—technophobia. This message reinforces the point that people can learn to use technical equipment; they simply may have to look at things a little differently to be able to do it.

Jigsaw Puzzles

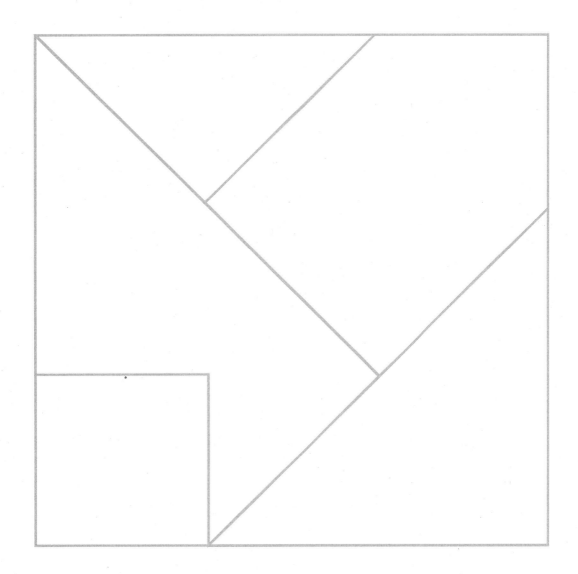

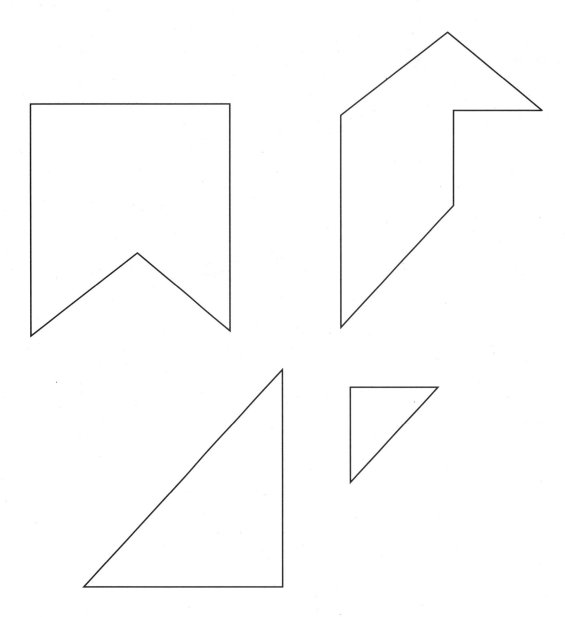

Can you arrange the above four pieces into a rectangle?

Warming Up the Crowd! by Dave Arch and Rich Meiss.
Copyright © 2000 by Jossey-Bass/Pfeiffer and Creative Training Techniques Press, San Francisco, CA.

Four-Piece Jigsaw

Preparation

Duplicate the opposite page so that each participant can have a copy. Provide scissors for each person. Participants will race to be the first one done in this challenging activity.

Solution

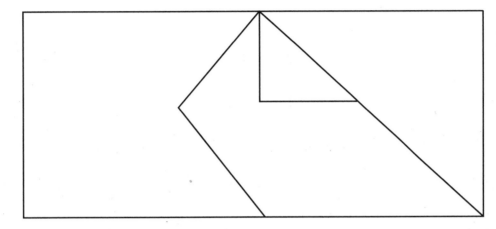

Application

Before starting the race, have each person print a key idea from the previous session on each puzzle piece. After sharing those ideas with other members of their table team, the challenge is then to "put it all together."

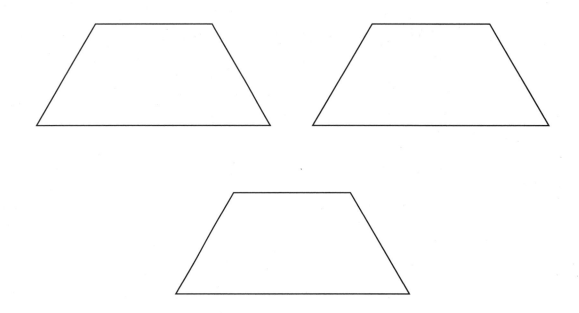

Can you use the above three pieces to make a large triangle? No overlapping, cutting, or folding of pieces allowed!

Three-Piece Jigsaw

Preparation

Duplicate the opposite page so that each participant can have a copy.

Solution

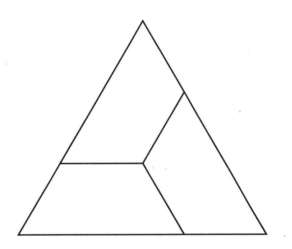

Application

Start off a multiple-day training session with this activity. Use it as a method of reviewing by having each person print, on each piece, a key component they remember from the day before. After they share their recollections, use the puzzle to emphasize how difficult it can sometimes be to "put together" those components. However, persistence does pay off!

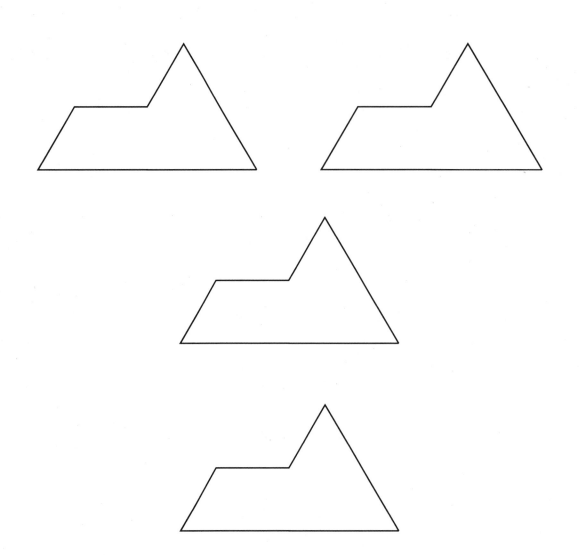

Use the four pieces above to make an even larger sphinx of the same shape! No cutting, overlapping, or folding allowed!

Sphinx Jigsaw

Preparation

Duplicate the opposite page so that each participant can have a copy. Each person will also need scissors.

Solution

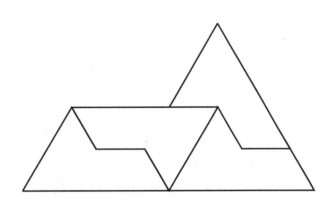

Application

Use this jigsaw puzzle as a review or use it as an opener. Ask participants to write on each piece a question that they would like to have answered before the session is over. Once they have shared their questions with others at their table, ask them to attempt to solve the Mystery of the Sphinx. That's what the session will be about . . . solving the mystery of their questions!

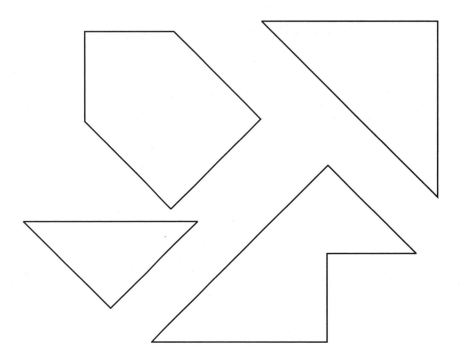

Can you use the above four pieces to make a square like the one below?

Sure you can!

Four-Piece Puzzler

Preparation

Copy the opposite page so that each person can have a copy. Participants will also need a pair of scissors.

Solution

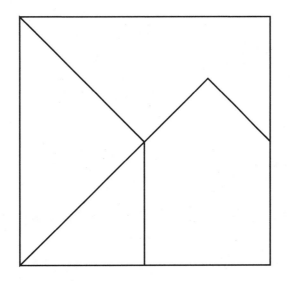

Application

Persistence is crucial to solving any problem. What are the components that caused some members of the group to just plain give up?

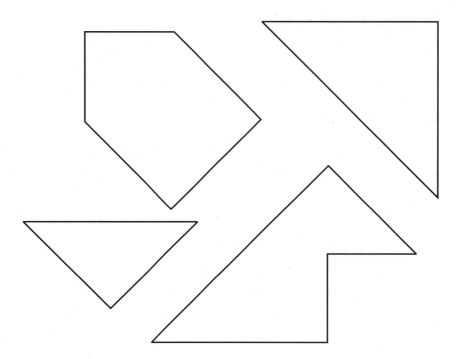

Can you use all five pieces (including the little square piece below) to make a large square?

Sure you can!

Five-Piece Puzzler

Preparation

Copy the opposite page so that each person can have a copy. They will also need a pair of scissors.

Solution

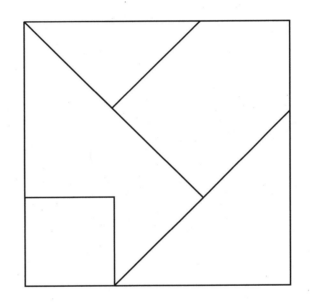

Application

Anytime we insert a new piece of information into an established system or process, we need to rearrange the other pieces to make room for it. It always takes a little time to incorporate the new piece into the total operation. This puzzle and its four-piece companion puzzle illustrate that point graphically. They are perfect to use anytime an organization is going through change.

Find-a-Words

N	S	G	P	U	G	N	I	M	R	A	W	O	L	S
A	O	S	A	C	R	L	P	W	O	R	C	E	H	T
T	A	R	I	D	I	A	G	O	N	A	L	L	Y	A
S	C	A	R	E	L	F	M	E	W	H	Y	V	O	C
H	O	H	T	E	M	L	I	G	O	S	Z	A	M	K
E	U	A	E	S	N	J	D	N	R	S	H	L	D	S
Q	T	L	K	R	O	E	X	B	D	E	C	A	T	R
U	P	I	L	E	S	T	O	P	S	N	E	K	I	M
I	L	C	I	A	W	E	H	M	I	G	P	U	L	E
L	Z	A	R	C	J	T	R	A	T	S	U	C	Q	E
T	R	E	V	L	L	Q	A	I	E	X	K	N	T	V
L	H	P	U	Z	Z	L	E	S	I	B	D	E	F	M
Y	A	B	A	E	K	D	I	M	C	R	I	C	E	A
S	D	R	A	W	K	C	A	B	H	C	R	A	E	S

Find the words listed at the bottom among these letters, and circle the words. They might be vertical, diagonal, horizontal, forwards, or backwards.

```
Y Z F E H B A V I S I O N L W
M T R L W U T B V R K B T F O
H P I H S R E D A E L W V G X
R G E L Q E A C L W A I E M E
H E N N I G M H U O C F E E L
W A D I V B S A E L X W T P E
R V S I D V I R S L O O X Z Z
T V H J V N R S D O A G E K E
G V I C V E O T N F R N M L M
P K P F G T R B I O U V P B T
I X I A S U T S U N P Z O J T
C K N I S B X P I G M S W O E
A A W T O F L T O T G M E F L
M P X F B Y Y R W B Y K R R P
```

Bonding	**Followers**	**Manager**	**Unity**
Boss	**Friendship**	**Responsibility**	**Values**
Diversity	**Group**	**Teams**	**Vision**
Empower	**Leadership**	**Trust**	

Leadership

Preparation

Make a copy of the master on the opposite page.

Solution

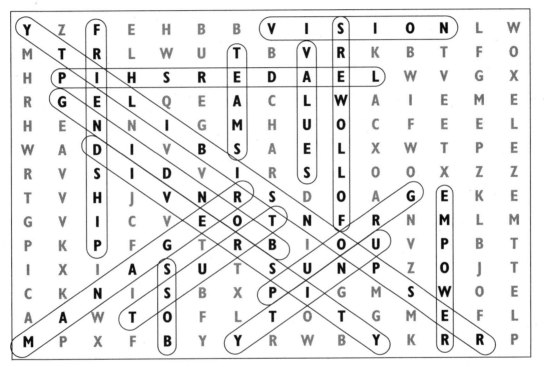

Application

Look closely to find the important aspects of leadership. Utilize the power of working together as a team to solve the find-a-word more quickly.

Find-a-word software called Crosswords and More™ is available from Creative Training Techniques Press at 1-800-383-9210, or may be accessed on the web at www.puzzlemaker.com.

Find the words listed at the bottom among these letters, and circle the words. They might be vertical, diagonal, horizontal, forwards, or backwards.

```
H E D E T A M I N A T N E I T A P
G O G J G A A S S E R T I V E C O
U V A R G L D P S U O R O G I V G
O E G V N H M V S S E L T S E R N
R T N S I S T O E V M S Q X Z L I
O A I L D M D G D N T A W X H A R
H R M A N C O M P E T I T I V E I
T U R N A A V M A N R U B A V D P
E C A O T M D D D V C A R I E E S
P C H I S I Y E E E C V T O E C N
I A C T R A T H L I T I D E U I I
O K Y O E B F V T I S N G Z U S K
N A J M D L R S V N B T E S J I T
E A S E N E I E E J L E F T S V W
E Y W L U M V S T Q T J R G N E X
R U V I I S U O I R E S P A F O M
I X P T E V I T A K L A T N T T C
N O P O C I T A M O L P I D F E K
G O S S U O I T U A C T R G X I S
P E R S U A S I V E S I C E R P W
```

Accurate   Competitive   Moderate   Sensitive
Adventurous   Contented   Optimistic   Serious
Amiable   Decisive   Patient   Steady
Animated   Deliberate   Persuasive   Talkative
Assertive   Diplomatic   Pioneering   Thorough
Cautious   Emotional   Precise   Understanding
Charming   Inspiring   Restless   Vigorous

Motivation: Personality

Preparation

Make a copy of the master on the opposite page.

Solution

```
H  E  D  E  T  A  M  I  N  A  T  N  E  I  T  A  P
G  O  G  J  G  A  A  S  S  E  R  T  I  V  E  C  O
U  V  A  R  G  L  D  P  S  U  O  R  O  G  I  V  G
O  E  G  V  N  H  M  V  S  S  E  L  T  S  E  R  N
R  T  N  S  I  S  T  O  E  V  M  S  Q  X  Z  L  I
O  A  I  L  D  M  D  G  D  N  T  A  W  X  H  A  R
H  R  M  A  N  C  O  M  P  E  T  I  T  I  V  E  I
T  U  R  N  A  A  V  M  A  N  R  U  B  A  V  D  P
E  C  A  O  T  M  D  D  D  V  C  A  R  I  E  E  S
P  C  H  I  S  I  Y  E  E  E  C  V  T  O  E  C  N
I  A  C  T  R  A  T  H  L  I  T  I  D  E  U  I  I
O  K  Y  O  E  B  F  V  T  I  S  N  G  Z  U  S  K
N  A  J  M  D  L  R  S  V  N  B  T  E  S  J  I  T
E  A  S  E  N  E  I  E  E  J  L  E  F  T  S  V  W
E  Y  W  L  U  M  V  S  T  Q  T  J  R  G  N  E  X
R  U  V  I  I  S  U  O  I  R  E  S  P  A  F  O  M
I  X  P  T  E  V  I  T  A  K  L  A  T  N  T  T  C
N  O  P  O  C  I  T  A  M  O  L  P  I  D  F  E  K
G  O  S  S  U  O  I  T  U  A  C  T  R  G  X  I  S
P  E  R  S  U  A  S  I  V  E  S  I  C  E  R  P  W
```

Application

Sometimes we have to look extra carefully to see all the positive qualities in other people. Use this pre-class warmup when doing any type of personality assessment, such as the Myers-Briggs Type Indicator (MBTI), the Personal Profile System (DISC), or Social Styles.

Find the words listed at the bottom among these letters, and circle the words. They might be vertical, diagonal, horizontal, forwards, or backwards.

```
N  M  I  E  O  F  X  F  K  O  J  W  C  L  R
O  O  C  J  G  B  E  N  E  F  I  T  S  E  T
I  D  I  S  A  B  I  L  I  T  Y  P  T  R  V
T  A  P  T  P  T  B  Z  H  E  A  I  A  U  V
A  N  F  X  A  Y  N  I  G  P  R  C  N  D  B
N  O  E  I  J  S  P  E  E  E  S  O  D  E  N
I  I  O  M  R  W  N  R  M  G  T  U  A  C  D
M  T  E  U  Y  I  W  E  O  S  Q  E  R  O  G
I  A  U  T  M  O  N  A  P  T  S  J  D  R  N
R  C  Y  P  R  T  L  G  B  M  O  A  S  P  I
C  A  K  K  S  R  P  X  D  O  C  R  L  R
S  V  I  C  Q  Y  Z  U  M  Q  B  C  O  A  I
I  L  L  N  E  S  S  B  I  E  J  B  B  L  H
D  K  O  X  M  I  S  S  I  O  N  E  G  F  L
N  Q  P  G  G  W  P  D  V  A  H  U  Y  K  Q
```

Benefits	Goals	Paperwork	Standards
Compensation	Harassment	Policy	Unemployment
Disability	Hiring	Procedure	Vacation
Discrimination	Illness	Protocol	
Firing	Mission	Retirement	

New-Employee Orientation

Preparation

Make a copy from the master on the opposite page.

Solution

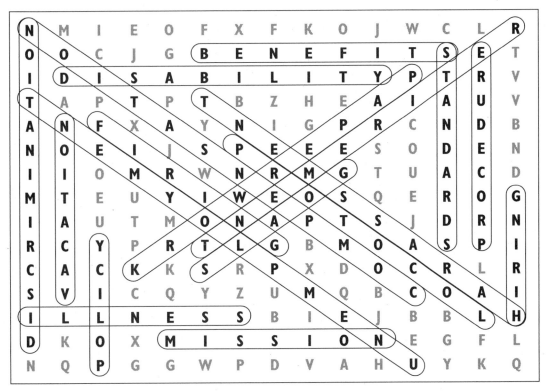

Application

To get the most from your new job at an organization, you will need to be alert for some things that might appear hidden. You will also want to be alert for some things to avoid.

Section **5**

Board Games

Directions

Above you see two cages. However, as you can see, there is still an animal loose. Cut out the eight black fence pieces above and arrange them on your table so that you make three cages using only the eight fence pieces.

Then, if you cut out the animals, you should be able to drop one inside each cage. You are not allowed to fold, bend, twist, tear, or break any of the fence pieces.

Cagey

Preparation

Duplicate the opposite page so that you can put one at each participant's place. Participants will also need a pair of scissors.

Solution

Application

Often we are forced to get more work done with our existing resources (such as time, budgets, and personnel), which takes creativity to accomplish. This activity dramatically demonstrates the possibility of getting more done with the same resources. It can easily begin a great discussion.

After cutting out the five letter-blocks, arrange them in a single row so that they spell a very common English word. No proper names allowed!

Baffling Blocks

Preparation

Duplicate the opposite page so that each person receives one copy. Each person will also need a pair of scissors.

Solution

CAMEL

Application

Getting trapped by rules of our own making is the quickest way to become ineffective in a problem solving situation. No one said that the letters could not be turned on their side or even upside down, which is exactly what you'll need to do to solve this puzzle.

This application can lead toward many other types of applications, all of which involve the process of creativity in problem solving and the role of our own assumptions in hindering that process.

2	9	4
7	5	3
6	1	8

Directions

Two people play this game. One person uses pennies as markers and one uses nickels. Taking turns, each person must cover a number when it is his or her turn. The first person to cover numbers totaling exactly fifteen, using three of their coins, wins! (More than three of their coins may be in play when this finally occurs.)

Carnival Countdown

Preparation

Duplicate the opposite page so that each person receives one copy. You might also have some pennies and nickels on the table, so that people can read the instructions and play the game while waiting for the class to begin.

Solution

This game is not what it first appears. Actually, the winner will be the one who figures out that it is really a game of tic-tac-toe with coins. In other words, the first person who gets three coins in a row (horizontally, diagonally, or vertically) will win.

Application

Anyone not spending sufficient time analyzing a situation will always be at a disadvantage. To emphasize this point, have the following message printed on small slips of paper: "You are really playing a game of tic-tac-toe. Try to be the first person to get your three coins in a row horizontally, vertically, or diagonally. You'll win."

After several games have been played, hand these little slips out so that only one person in each group of two players gets to see the message. Then ask them to play another game. The information you share with the one player will put him or her at an advantage over the other player.

That's exactly what you as a trainer will be doing in your session—sharing insights that will help each participant be a winner in his or her career. Knowledge is power!

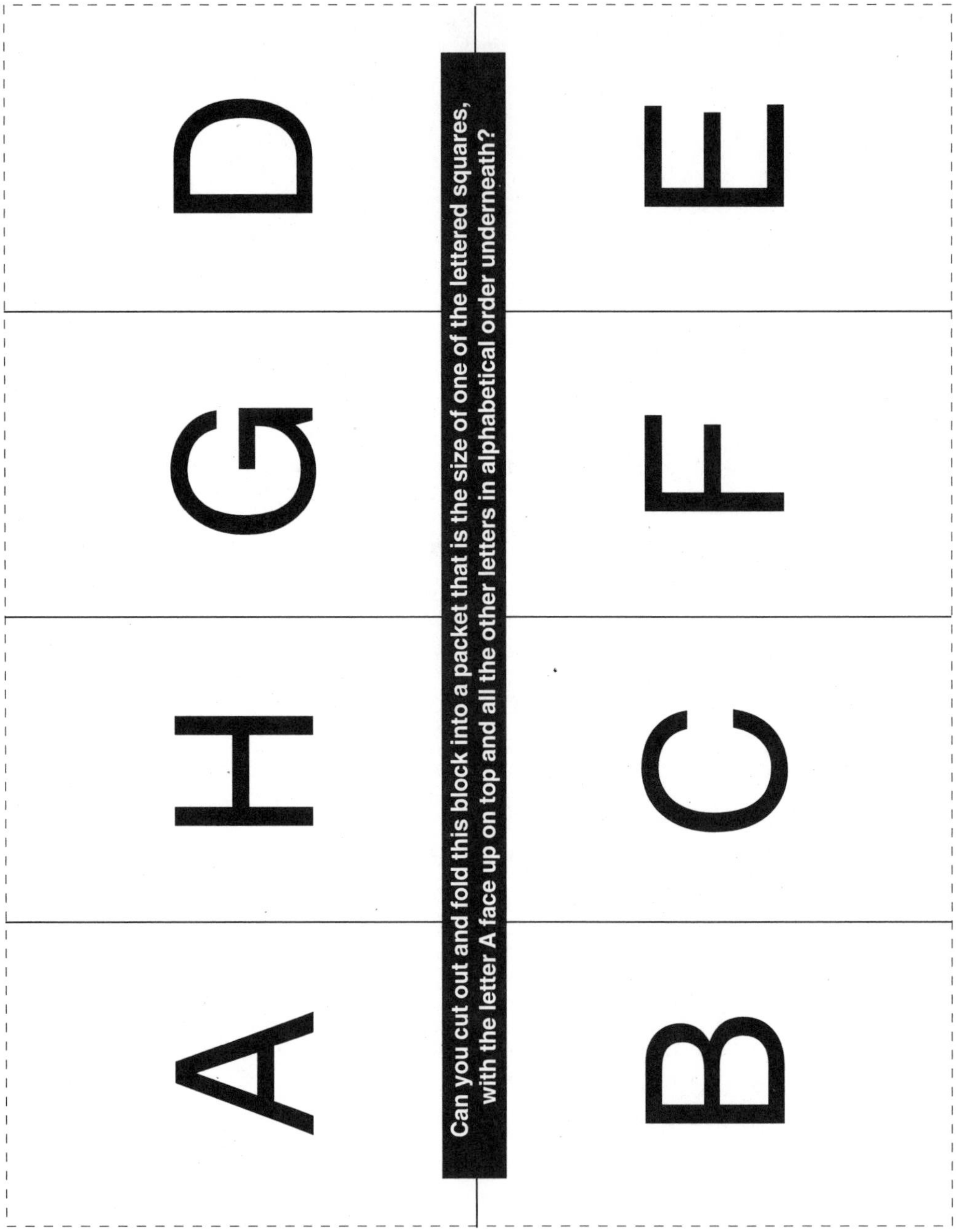
Can you cut out and fold this block into a packet that is the size of one of the lettered squares,
with the letter A face up on top and all the other letters in alphabetical order underneath?
D
E
G
F
H
C
A
B

Letter Fold

Preparation

Duplicate the opposite page so that you can place one at each participant's place. Provide scissors for each table. When participants come in and sit down, they can attempt to solve the puzzle. Be sure they cut the puzzle out first.

Solution

1. Hold the sheet of paper face down with the A and B in your left hand and the D and E in your right hand.

2. Fold the sheet in half, right to left, with squares D and E coming over on top of squares A and B.

3. Now fold it in half, from bottom to top, with the letters A and H coming up to the top of the packet.

4. Tuck squares D and E (as a single unit) in between squares C and F.

5. Finally, fold squares A and B so that A shows on top of the packet.

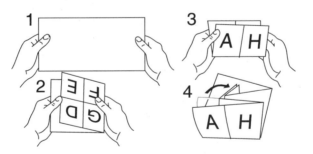

Application

What process did each person use to try to solve the problem? The approach each person uses (trial and error, careful analysis, or such) is typically the approach that person takes in solving the problems he or she faces.

What are the benefits of each approach? The liabilities?

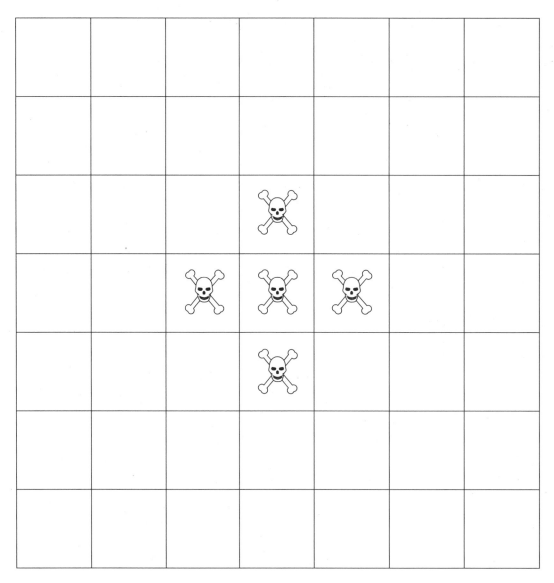

Print seven (7) X's into the squares on the grid (one X per box) so that no X is in the same row as any other X either vertically, horizontally, or diagonally.

If you find that too easy, then try to accomplish the task without placing any of the X's in the squares marked by the skulls!

Skullduggery

Preparation

Duplicate the opposite page so that each participant can have a copy. If you make this an activity in which teams compete with each other to be the first to solve the puzzle, you will add even more energy to this activity.

Solution

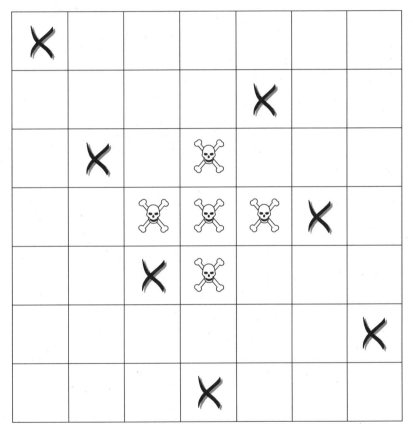

Application

Customize the puzzle by replacing the skulls with words that reflect aspects of an organization that participants will want to avoid (for example, low-quality product, poor customer service, missed deadlines). Then participants could print seven words that reflect positive aspects instead of using the X's.

You have both a review tool and energizer in one!

Cut out the following pieces of snake and try to arrange them into a snake biting its tail.

Snake Eyes

Preparation

Duplicate the opposite page so that each person in your group can have one. Provide scissors for each table. Then put the following instructions on your overhead projector.

"Cut out the pieces of snake and try to arrange them into a snake biting its tail."

Solution

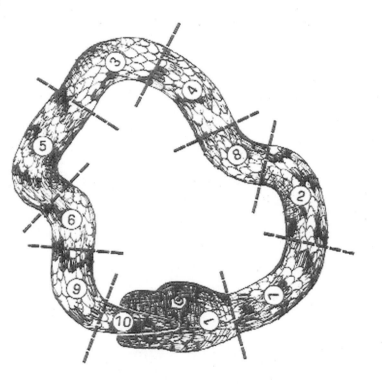

Application

This exercise underscores the role of persistence in achieving any goal. How many wrong solutions did each person need to try before finding a correct solution? How impossible would this have been if participants had merely attempted to look at the pieces without trying some possibilities? These questions and others will guide the group to some applicational reminders that help us all cope with the problems around us in both our business and personal lives.

Player #2 **START**

2	2	4	11	15	20	21
4	1	1	6	13	18	19
11	6	3	3	8	14	17
15	13	8	5	5	12	16
20	18	14	12	9	9	10
21	19	17	16	10	7	7

Player #1 **START** (left side) · Player #1 **FINISH** (right side)

Player #2 **FINISH**

Directions

Two people begin play by selecting either X's or O's as their symbol and then taking turns marking their X's or O's in the above squares.

The goal is to form a connected path of your symbols. Player 1 moves from the left side of the game board to the right side, before Player 2 can form a connected path with his or her symbols from the top of the game board to the bottom.

The path may be crooked or straight. You are allowed to block your opponent's path when it's your turn. Obviously, the shorter the path, the better your chances of winning. Good luck!

Warming Up the Crowd! by Dave Arch and Rich Meiss.
Copyright © 2000 by Jossey-Bass/Pfeiffer and Creative Training Techniques Press, San Francisco, CA.

The Race

Preparation

Copy the opposite page and distribute a copy to each participant. They can then play while you're getting ready to begin your training session. Promise them that you will share with them a strategy that always wins the game. This will raise their curiosity as they envision themselves using the game with other people.

Solution

You will always win the race if you are Player 2 and you parrot the moves of your opponent. In other words, if the opponent puts an X in square 15 to start, you put your O in the other square 15. By sticking to this strategy, you will always win!

Application

It's amazing what a carefully planned strategy can accomplish. However, it is not enough to devise the strategy—it must also be followed. Keep those two thoughts in mind so that you can use this activity to make the transition into any content area that involves a process—one that must be followed to achieve success.

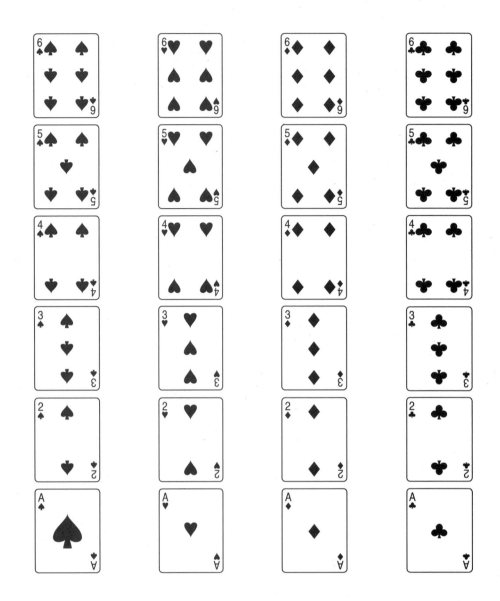

Directions

Two people play this ancient game by taking turns crossing out cards from the diagram above. Each card's numerical value is added to the sum of the cards already crossed out. The person who wins is the one who crosses out the card that makes the sum total 31. If anyone crosses out a card that causes the total to exceed 31, that person loses!

Thirty-One

Preparation

You'll need to copy the diagram on the opposite page so that everyone in your group can have at least five (depending on how many times you wish them to play). You might also make a transparency of the chart so that you can show on the overhead the strategies that make winning possible.

Solution

After they've tried a few games, give them the following strategy.

The strategy is to hit the total of 17 or 24 on your turn. If you can hit 17 or 24 when it's your turn, you'll win for sure. Try that strategy and see how it works. However, even when this strategy is known by your opponent, you can still win. Begin by crossing out one of the aces. Let your opponent take his or her turn and then you cross out another ace. After your opponent's next turn, you cross out the third ace and finally the fourth ace. Your opponent will have hit 17 without a struggle, and then 24. When the other person hits 24, you will have crossed out all four aces and then you must cross out a 6—bringing the total to 30. The other person will suddenly realize that all the aces have been crossed out and there is no choice but to cross out a higher card—exceeding 31 and therefore going "bust."

Application

The exercise shows clearly that just because, at one time, we believed that a certain strategy was "best" for the company, that it must continue to be the "best." As information increases (and markets change), new "bests" present themselves, and change is inevitable if we are to continue winning in sales or any other endeavor.

Tangram Tricks

Introduction to Tangrams

This fascinating Chinese game called tangrams began in China around 1800 and then spread rapidly westward. There are over 1600 design possibilities that can be constructed with one seven-piece set. Tangrams were puzzle pieces originally made from finely engraved ivory or mother-of-pearl. However you're sure to find that cut-out pieces of paper work just fine, too.

Trainers are finding tangrams to be excellent pre-session activities. They use them in three distinct manners:

1. Trainers encourage table teams to discover and create the most fascinating content-related figures straight from their own imaginations. Then those figures can be displayed on a separate table in the room for others to enjoy.

2. Trainers show figures on the overhead in outline form only and challenge the teams to be the first to create the figure from the seven pieces of their tangram set.

3. Trainers introduce to the group timed challenges wherein teams try to be the first to create specifically assigned figures without the help of any outlines.

You'll find the latter two of those applications reflected in the activities that follow.

Cut apart the pieces and try to use them to form the dancers that you see printed beneath the pieces.

Warming Up the Crowd! by Dave Arch and Rich Meiss.

Tangram Teaser 1

Preparation

Copy the opposite page and distribute to each person (or table team) in your training class. Each person will also need a pair of scissors.

Solution

See the patterns under the pieces on the facing page.

Application

Use tangrams in this manner when you want to illustrate some differences between individual effort and team effort. First let individual participants try the patterns, and then let them tackle the task in teams. Discuss the differences in both positive and negative terms.

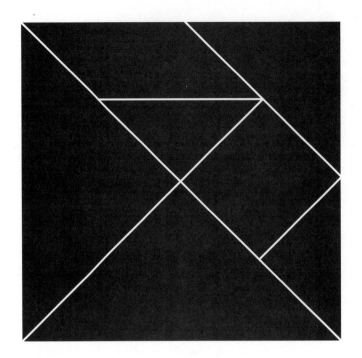

Can you use all seven of your tangram pieces to make the following?

1. A House

2. A Plant

3. A Bird

4. A Lion

5. A Sailboat

6. A Knife

7. Your Initials

8. Numerals from 0-9

9. A Human Figure Sitting

10. A Human Figure Running

11. A Human Figure Falling

12. Three Geometric Figures

Tangram Teaser 2

Preparation

Copy the opposite page onto a transparency master to introduce the exercise to your participants. You might also consider making the solutions into a transparency too. It is assumed that each participant already has the tangram pieces from a previous activity.

Solutions

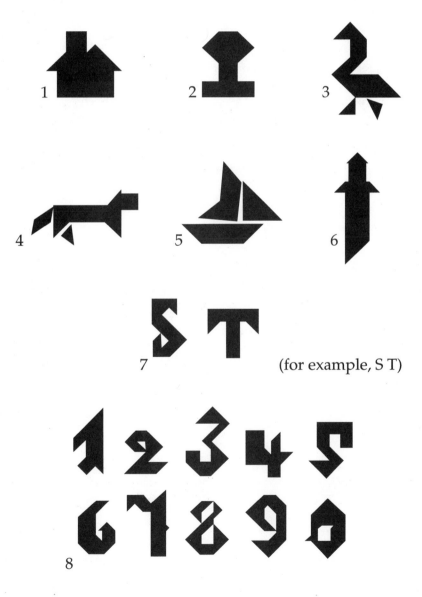

(for example, S T)

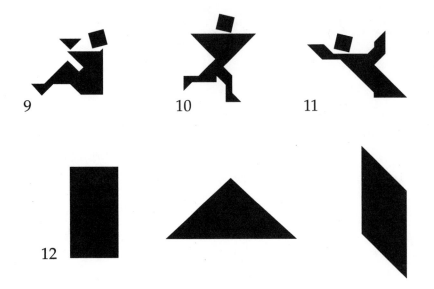

Application

Participants can have their set of tangram pieces with them all day long, and following each break you can challenge them with yet another figure from the list. Using this method you can get as many as twelve different pre-session activities from this one concept! Introduce it as a timed exercise, and the first person or table team accomplishing the task wins a prize. Have the winner(s) come to the front and build the figure on the overhead so everyone can see just how to make it.

You can also have key concepts printed on the backs of the pieces to highlight parts of your presentation, or use them as we did in the Jigsaw Puzzle sections as a review of subject matter by having participants share and write their own memorable components from the course on the various pieces.

Crossword Puzzle

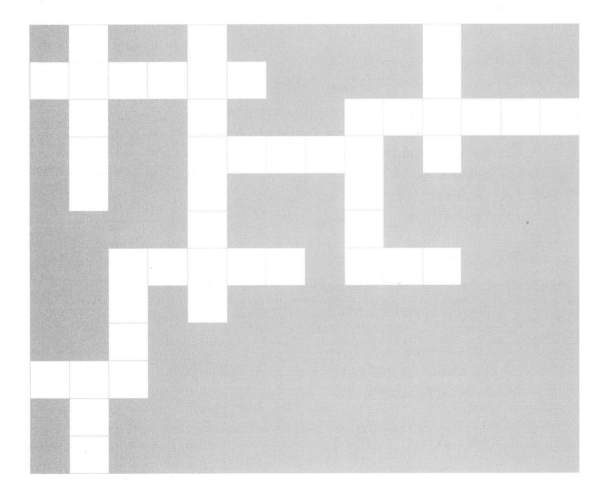

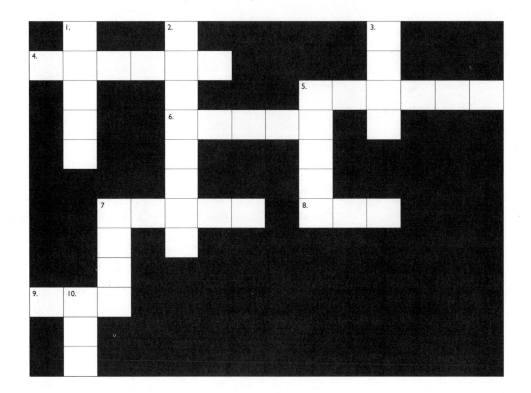

Across

4. A file used to store and organize documents
5. A message requesting the user's response
6. American Standard Code for Information Interchange
7. A process method in which a program records with little or no operator action
8. Local Area Network
9. Cathode Ray Tube Display

Down

1. Device that connects computers to phone lines
2. About one million bytes
3. A graphic symbol displayed on a screen
5. Picture element
7. To load an operating system
10. Random Access Memory

Computer Crossword Puzzle

Preparation

Make a handout from the master on the opposite page.

Solution

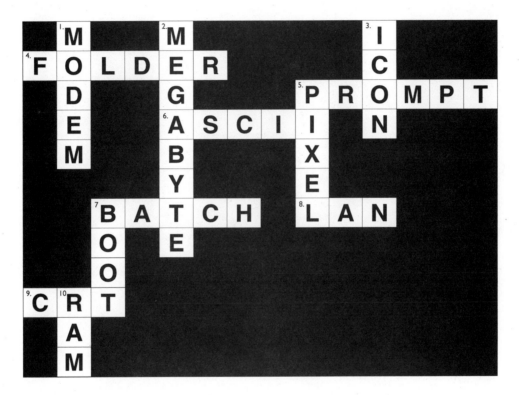

Application

Use crossword puzzles as a pre-class warm-up activity to help acquaint participants with class content. Crossword puzzles are also useful to review content activity.

To build your own crossword puzzles easily with inexpensive computer software, Crosswords and More™ software is available from Creative Training Techniques Press at 1-800-383-9210. You can also access crossword software on the Web at: www.puzzlemaker.com or www. shareware.com.

Section 8

Calculator Fun

Introduction to Calculator Fun

These innovative pre-session activities are based on the fact that certain numbers on older-model calculators (as well as on some newer ones) appear as letters when inverted. Following is a chart of numbers and their corresponding inverted letter:

1 = I	4 = H	8 = B
2 = Z	5 = S	9 = G
3 = E	7 = L	0 = O

The numbers on most of the newer calculators, as well as on some of the older ones, aren't as "blocky" and consequently don't work for this demonstration. That should not be a problem because there are many of the older calculators still in circulation. Or the trainer might simply plan on using his or her own calculator for the demonstration.

As you can see from that letter listing, there are numerous possible combinations. See the word list on page 97 for more ideas. To familiarize yourself with this concept, take your calculator and work through the following examples:

I'm thinking of a city in Idaho. It has a population of 30,000 (so put that number in your calculator), the speed limit is 55 mph (so add the number 55 to your previous entry), the highest mountain in the state is 5,000 feet (so add 5,000 to your total), and the best steak dinner in this city costs 53 dollars (finally, add 53 to your total). Your inverted answer will tell you the city of which I'm thinking.

Here's another one:

The company is now using a new testing procedure to determine who's eligible for a position with the firm. Take a calculator and add the numbers 37 + 81 + 91 + 73. Does your answer look the same even when it's inverted? It should! Good. That's the eye test.

Now put the same numbers in the calculator without the plus (+) signs. You will have the numbers 37819173 on the screen. (This is only to see if you can follow directions.) Turn your calculator over to see if you're eligible for a position.

Try one more:

Assume for a moment that you made $938 per year. Enter that figure into a calculator and turn it upside down to see what you'd need to do in order to make ends meet. Let's assume you received a raise of $5055 for the year. Add that to your first figure to see what you could now afford to buy. Finally, add $26015 for the cost of your treatment if you begin to take in too much of this drink.

The activities in this Calculator Fun section can be used in several ways:

1. Duplicate the question sheet and have them at each participant's place as they enter the room. When you get ready to begin the session, go through participants' answer sheets and see how many they got right.
2. Call the questions out from the front of the room, giving prizes to the first person or team that calls out the answer.
3. Customize your own questions so that they correspond to your content.

When building a customized pre-session activity for your training content, follow these guidelines for maximum impact:

1. Give each number in the computation a reason for existing (such as the number of days in a year, the number of letters in the company's name, the phone number of a financial expert, and the like).
2. Using a series of computations with different clever words (such as "giggle," "slob," "boss," and so forth) makes the strongest impression. As each word changes into another word, the impact is heightened. Three changes seem to be the perfect number for this series.

3. Although the word list doesn't contain any proper names, several common ones are possible. If you have a participant with the name of Bill or Lee or Bob, by all means use it to personalize the closing.

4. Don't be afraid to combine words—adding a decimal point to separate the words.

The following words are some of those that can be made with the inverted numbers of a calculator. The required calculator number in parentheses follows the word.

BE (38)
BEE (338)
BEIGE (39138)
BELL (7738)
BESIEGE (3931538)
BIG (918)
BILL (7718)
BLISS (55178)
BOGGLE (379908)
BOIL (7108)
BOOZE (32008)
BOSS (5508)
EEL (733)
EGG (993)
ELIGIBLE (37819173)
GEESE (35339)
GLEE (3379)
GOOSE (35009)
GIGGLE (379919)
GLIB (8179)
GLOB (8079)

GOBBLE (378809)
GOGGLES (5379909)
HELLISH (4517734)
HIGH (4914)
HOBBIES (5318804)
HOE (304)
HOGGISH (4519904)
HOLE (3704)
ILL (771)
ILLEGIBLE
    (378193771)
IS (51)
ISLE (3751)
LEG (937)
LEGIBLE (3781937)
LESS (5537)
LIBEL (73817)
LIE (317)
LILIES (531717)
LOG (907)
LOOSE (35007)

LOSE (3507)
LOSS (5507)
OBESE (35380)
OBLIGE (391780)
OIL (710)
SEE (335)
SEIZE (32135)
SELL (7735)
SHE (345)
SHELL (77345)
SHOE (3045)
SIEGE (39315)
SIGH (4915)
SIZE (3215)
SIZZLE (372215)
SLEIGH BELLS
    (57738.491375)
SLOB (8075)
SOB (805)
SOIL (7105)

1. The square root of 196 and get a greeting.

2. 44 × 70 and get a musical instrument.

3. 52,043 ÷ 71 and get a snake-like fish.

4. (30,000,000 − 2,457,433) × 2 and find out why a male president of a company gets his own way.

5. $7,964^2$ + 7,652,049 and get the name of a large oil company.

6. 711 × 10,000 − 9,447 and get a competing oil corporation.

7. (53.5149 − 51.4414) ÷ 29 and find a farmer's storage facility.

8. (15^2 − 124) × 5 and get a distress signal.

9. (2 − 1.4351) ÷ 7 and get a name for a wolf.

10. (159 × 357 − 19,025) and get a beautiful young lady.

11. 471 × 265 + 410,699 and learn what a snake does.

12. 99^2 − 2,087 and get a rise.

13. (1 − .930394) ÷ .9 and get a telephone greeting.

14. .161616 ÷ 4 and find out what Santa Claus said when you asked him for a yacht.

Warming Up the Crowd! by Dave Arch and Rich Meiss.
Copyright © 2000 by Jossey-Bass/Pfeiffer and Creative Training Techniques Press, San Francisco, CA.

Upside-Down Displays 1

Answers

1. HI
2. OBOE
3. EEL
4. HE IS BOSS
5. SHELL OIL
6. ESSO OIL
7. SILO
8. SOS
9. LOBO
10. BELLE
11. HISSES
12. HILL
13. HELLO
14. HOHOHO

1. 31 × 11 × 11 and get a small island.

2. 3^9 + 35,495 and get a description of married life.

3. 5,016 × 11 + 2,542 and get unwelcome arrivals on the first of the month.

4. 1,000 + 852.8667 × 2 and get the bottom line on your shoes.

5. 851^2 − 143,667 and find out what a man does when he loses a winning lottery ticket worth $100,000.

6. 0 − 1,234,567 + 6,589,945 and find what a preacher does.

7. 2,101 × 18 and get the name of a very good book.

8. 60^2 − 96 and get a gardening tool.

9. 1,234 − 463 and find out what you'll be after eating four gallons of ice cream.

10. 305,644 ÷ 43 and get into hot water.

11. 9,999 − 8,038 × 3 and find what the tide does after it flows.

12. 73^2 + 9 and get a honey of an answer.

13. 127^3 + 4,618,283 − 1,347,862 and find how people occupy their spare time.

Upside-Down Displays 2

Answers

1. ISLE
2. BLISS
3. BILLS
4. HEEL, SOLE
5. HE SOBS
6. BLESSES
7. BIBLE
8. HOSE
9. ILL
10. BOIL
11. EBBS
12. BEES
13. HOBBIES

1. 4 × 8,777 and get a city in Idaho.

2. The more you take away, the larger it grows. What is it? Square root of 13719616.

3. If bourbon whisky is $8 a bottle in Chicago, what is scotch in New York? (8 × 4001)

4. What did Dr. Livingstone say after Stanley said, "Dr. Livingstone, I presume?" (18 × 4, then ÷ 3 and the result decreased by 10)

5. Are there similar calculator stunts that use foreign words? Add 1 to the answer arrived at in number 4.

Upside-Down Displays 3

Answers

1. BOISE
2. HOLE
3. BOOZE
4. HI
5. SI

Mix and Match

Because many organizations are looking for kinder, gentler ways of describing people and things, they sometimes go overboard. Match the terms on the left with their more "subtle" versions on the right.

1. Lifestyle-downsizing opportunity	A.	drunk
2. Melanin-impoverished	B.	girl
3. Economically exploited	C.	mailman
4. Sobriety-deprived	D.	unemployment
5. Cerebrally challenged	E.	dead
6. Pre-woman	F.	white
7. Chronologically gifted	G.	manhole
8. Utility hole	H.	airhead
9. Person-box	I.	poor
10. Person-person	J.	mailbox
11. Involuntarily undomiciled	K.	homeless
12. Terminally disadvantaged	L.	stupid
13. Cerebrally atmospheric individual	M.	old

Warming Up the Crowd! by Dave Arch and Rich Meiss.
Copyright © 2000 by Jossey-Bass/Pfeiffer and Creative Training Techniques Press, San Francisco, CA.

New-Employee Orientation: Politically Correct Dictionary

Preparation

Make a copy of the master on the opposite page.

Solution

1. D—Unemployment—lifestyle-downsizing opportunity
2. F—Melanin-impoverished—white
3. I—Economically exploited—poor
4. A—Sobriety-deprived—drunk
5. L—Cerebrally challenged—stupid
6. B—Pre-woman—girl
7. M—Chronologically gifted—old
8. G—Utility hole—manhole
9. J—Person-box—mailbox
10. C—Person-person—mailman
11. K—Involuntarily undomiciled—homeless
12. E—Terminally disadvantaged—dead
13. H—Cerebrally atmospheric individual—airhead

Application

A respect for all people is a healthy trait, but let's not go too far in our desire to be politically correct. Have some fun with these rather silly examples.

Listed below are commonly used oxymorons. Fill in the blank at the left with a word that fits from the right column.

Example:

Pretty	_ugly_	vacation
Working	_vacation_	ugly

1. Nondairy	_____	landfill
2. Live	_____	benefits
3. Smokeless	_____	aggression
4. Great	_____	junkies
5. Perfect	_____	frozen
6. Unemployment	_____	crowd
7. Civil	_____	grief
8. Exercise	_____	imitation
9. Bottoms	_____	light
10. Shock	_____	maybe
11. No-fault	_____	creamer
12. Definite	_____	divorce
13. Fresh	_____	recording
14. Night	_____	up
15. Genuine	_____	tobacco
16. Good	_____	depression
17. Sanitary	_____	therapy
18. Legally	_____	jock
19. Small	_____	idiot
20. Passive	_____	misunderstood
21. Clearly	_____	war
22. Computer	_____	drunk

Warming Up the Crowd! by Dave Arch and Rich Meiss.
Copyright © 2000 by Jossey-Bass/Pfeiffer and Creative Training Techniques Press, San Francisco, CA.

Communication: Say What You Mean

Preparation

Make a handout from the master on the opposite page.

Solution

1. Nondairy creamer
2. Live recording
3. Smokeless tobacco
4. Great depression
5. Perfect idiot
6. Unemployment benefits
7. Civil war
8. Exercise junkies
9. Bottoms up
10. Shock therapy
11. No-fault divorce
12. Definite maybe
13. Fresh frozen
14. Night light
15. Genuine imitation
16. Good grief
17. Sanitary landfill
18. Legally drunk
19. Small crowd
20. Passive aggression
21. Clearly misunderstood
22. Computer jock

Application

Some things just don't fit together. Be careful in your communications to say what you mean, and then check for understanding. Clear communication is essential for excellent results. This would make an excellent energizer for communications classes, also.

Match the phrase on the left with its corresponding phrase on the right by drawing a line connecting the two.

It's Better to . . .   than to . . .

1. Reserve judgment   run around in circles.

2. Handle paper only once   beat your head against the wall.

3. Keep focused   jump on the bandwagon.

4. Use discretion   grasp at straws.

5. Get the job done   wade through the paperwork.

6. Keep your cool   drag your heels.

7. Communicate with reason   pass the buck.

8. Be patient   spin your wheels.

9. Affirm others   push your luck.

10. Help the cause   add fuel to the fire.

11. Listen with an open mind   throw your weight around.

12. Present a sound case   jump to conclusions.

13. Encourage others   climb the walls.

14. Empower others   fish for compliments.

15. Take responsibility   beat your own drum.

Warming Up the Crowd! by Dave Arch and Rich Meiss.
Copyright © 2000 by Jossey-Bass/Pfeiffer and Creative Training Techniques Press, San Francisco, CA.

Motivation: 15 Exercises We'd Be Better Off Without 69

Preparation

Make a copy of the master on the opposite page.

Solution

It's better to:

1. Reserve judgment   than to   jump on the bandwagon.
2. Handle paper only once   than to   wade through paperwork.
3. Keep focused   than to   run around in circles.
4. Use discretion   than to   push your luck.
5. Get the job done   than to   spin your wheels.
6. Keep your cool   than to   add fuel to the fire.
7. Communicate with reason   than to   beat your head against the wall.
8. Be patient   than to   climb the walls.
9. Affirm others   than to   beat your own drum.
10. Help the cause   than to   drag your heels.
11. Listen with an open mind   than to   jump to conclusions.
12. Present a sound case   than to   grasp at straws.
13. Encourage others   than to   fish for compliments.
14. Empower others   than to   throw your weight around.
15. Take responsibility   than to   pass the buck.

Application

"It's better to light one candle than to curse the darkness." Use these phrases to motivate people to positive action. In a seminar or meeting, have participants find the matching phrases by drawing lines across the page. They may then pick a favorite phrase and read it aloud. Continue until all participants have shared or all the phrases have been read. If time permits, an application idea or insight from an individual phrase may also be shared.

Suggestion: Use these as an energizer in long meetings or multiple-day training sessions.

Fill in the words below that match the "fun" computer definitions.

Examples:

<u>Batch</u>   The new chickens you just received.

<u>Prompt</u>   What you'd better be if you want supper.

1. _____ What you did to the hayfields.
2. _____ Where you hang your keys.
3. _____ What to shut when it's below zero.
4. _____ What to put on the stove when implementing Windows.
5. _____ Getting home in a January snowstorm.
6. _____ Getting the firewood out of the pickup.
7. _____ What you get if you're not careful downloading.
8. _____ What the calves leave in the pasture.
9. _____ What you say when you're calling your dog "Puter" to dinner.
10. _____ What Puter does when you don't feed him.
11. _____ What Puter does when you really make him mad.
12. _____ What you wear on your foot.
13. _____ What you drive when you're taking lots of folks.

Batch	**Crash**	**Megabyte**
Boot	**Download**	**Megahertz**
Bus	**Hard drive**	**Microchips**
Byte	**Keyboard**	**Modem**
Computer	**Log on**	**Prompt**

Warming Up the Crowd! by Dave Arch and Rich Meiss.
Copyright © 2000 by Jossey-Bass/Pfeiffer and Creative Training Techniques Press, San Francisco, CA.

Computers: Just for Fun—A Farmer's Definition of Terms

Preparation

Make a handout from the master on the opposite page.

Solution

1. Modem—What you did to the hayfields.
2. Keyboard—Where you hang your keys.
3. Windows—What to shut when it's below zero.
4. Log on—What to put on the stove when implementing Windows.
5. Hard drive—Getting home in a January snowstorm.
6. Download—Getting the firewood out of the pickup.
7. Megahertz—What you get if you're not careful downloading.
8. Microchips—What the calves leave in the pasture.
9. Computer—What you say when you're calling your dog "Puter" to dinner.
10. Byte—What Puter does when you don't feed him.
11. Megabyte—What Puter does when you really make him mad.
12. Boot—What you wear on your foot.
13. Bus—What you drive when you're taking lots of folks.

Application

Just for fun.

Fill in the Blanks

Below are euphemisms for 16 National Football Conference football teams. Can you and your team come up with the right 16 team names?

1. Seven squared   _____

2. Disrobes   _____

3. American gouchos   _____

4. Before they were Popes   _____

5. King of beasts   _____

6. A dollar for corn   _____

7. Hot epidermis   _____

8. Helpers to relocate   _____

9. Holy ones   _____

10. Army ants   _____

11. Birds trained to kill   _____

12. Six rulers   _____

13. Opposite of ewes   _____

14. Class of Boy Scouts   _____

15. Slacks for women   _____

16. Tans the skins   _____

Fun Warmups: Football Teams

Preparation

Make a handout from the master on the opposite page.

Solution

1.	Seven squared	49ers
2.	Disrobes	Bears
3.	American gouchos	Cowboys
4.	Before they were Popes	Cardinals
5.	King of beasts	Lions
6.	A dollar for corn	Buccaneers
7.	Hot epidermis	Redskins
8.	Helpers to relocate	Packers
9.	Holy ones	Saints
10.	Army ants	Giants (G.I. ants)
11.	Birds trained to kill	Falcons
12.	Six rulers	Vikings ([Roman numeral] VI kings)
13.	Opposite of Ewes	Rams
14.	Class of Boy Scouts	Eagles
15.	Slacks for women	Panthers
16.	Tans the Skins	Browns

Application

A warmup activity for fun. Use it during the football season or anytime for groups of sports enthusiasts. This activity is also a great energizer!

Below are euphemisms for 15 American Football Conference teams. Can you and your team come up with the right 15 team names?

1. Several 747's _____

2. Hostile attackers _____

3. Credit card users _____

4. Indian leaders _____

5. Looters _____

6. Used to be girls _____

7. Birds like crows _____

8. Ocean-going birds _____

9. IOU's _____

10. Toy baby with arms _____

11. Rodeo horses _____

12. Six-shooters _____

13. Paul Revere's friends _____

14. Race of gods _____

15. Pricey cars _____

Warming Up the Crowd! by Dave Arch and Rich Meiss.
Copyright © 2000 by Jossey-Bass/Pfeiffer and Creative Training Techniques Press, San Francisco, CA.

Fun Warmups:
More Football Teams

Preparation

Make a handout from the master on the opposite page.

Solution

1.	Several 747's	Jets
2.	Hostile attackers	Raiders
3.	Credit card users	Chargers
4.	Indian leaders	Chiefs
5.	Looters	Steelers
6.	Used to be girls	Bengals (Been gals)
7.	Birds like crows	Ravens
8.	Ocean-going birds	Seahawks
9.	IOU's	Bills
10.	Toy baby with arms	Dolphins (Doll fins)
11.	Rodeo horses	Broncos
12.	Six shooters	Colts
13.	Paul Revere's friends	Patriots
14.	Race of gods	Titans
15.	Pricey cars	Jaguars

Application

A warmup just for fun to use during the football season or anytime with sports enthusiasts. This activity is also a real energizer!

After much careful research it has been discovered that the artist Vincent van Gogh had many relatives. Write in the correct name from the list at the bottom of the page to match the correct description.

Examples:

| His grandfather from Yugoslavia | Yu Gogh |
| His little nephew | Po Gogh |

1. His obnoxious brother _____
2. The brother who worked at a convenience store _____
3. The brother who bleached his clothes white _____
4. The cousin from Illinois _____
5. His magician uncle _____
6. The nephew who drove a stagecoach _____
7. The ballroom-dancing aunt _____
8. The bird-lover uncle _____
9. His nephew psychoanalyst _____
10. The fruit-loving cousin _____
11. An aunt who taught positive thinking _____
12. A sister who loved disco _____
13. His niece who travels in a van _____

Chica Gogh
Hue Gogh
Winniebay Gogh
E. Gogh
Flamin Gogh

Go Gogh
Man Gogh
Please Gogh
Stop 'n' Gogh
Tan Gogh

Wayto Gogh
Wellsfar Gogh
Wherediddy Gogh

Fun Warmups:
The Van Gogh Family Tree

Preparation

Make a handout from the master on the opposite page.

Solution

1.	His obnoxious brother	Please Gogh
2.	The brother who worked at a convenience store	Stop 'n' Gogh
3.	The brother who bleached his clothes white	Hue Gogh
4.	The cousin from Illinois	Chica Gogh
5.	His magician uncle	Wherediddy Gogh
6.	The nephew who drove a stage coach	Wellsfar Gogh
7.	The ballroom-dancing aunt	Tan Gogh
8.	The bird-lover uncle	Flamin Gogh
9.	His nephew psychoanalyst	E. Gogh
10.	The fruit-loving cousin	Man Gogh
11.	An aunt who taught positive thinking	Wayto Gogh
12.	A sister who loved disco	Go Gogh
13.	His niece who travels in a van	Winniebay Gogh

Application

Just for fun!

Each item below contains the initials of words that will make it correct. Find the missing words.

Example:

16   O. in a P. = Ounces in a Pound.

26	L. of the A.	_____
7	W. of the A.W.	_____
1001	A.N.	_____
12	S. of the Z.	_____
54	C. in a D. (with the J.)	_____
9	P. in the S.S.	_____
88	P.K.	_____
13	S. on the A.F.	_____
32	D.F. at which W.F.	_____
18	H. on a G.C.	_____
90	D. in a R.A.	_____
200	D. for P.G. in M.	_____
8	S. on a S.S.	_____
3	B.M. (S.H.T.R.)	_____
4	Q. in a G.	_____
24	H. in a D.	_____
1	W. on a U.	_____
9	D. in a Z.C.	_____
57	H.V.	_____
11	P. on a F.T.	_____
1000	W. that a P. is W.	_____
29	D. in F. in a L.Y.	_____
64	S. on a C.B.	_____
40	D. and N. of the G.F.	_____
4	S. and S.Y.A.	_____

Initials Exercise

Preparation

Make a handout from the master on the opposite page.

Solution

26   Letters of the Alphabet

7   Wonders of the Ancient World

1001   Arabian Nights

12   Signs of the Zodiac

54   Cards in the Deck (with the Joker)

9   Planets in the Solar System

88   Piano Keys

13   Stripes on the American Flag

32   Degrees Fahrenheit at which Water Freezes

18   Holes on a Golf Course

90   Degrees in a Right Angle

200   Dollars for Passing Go in Monopoly

8   Sides on a Stop Sign (or Shrimp on a Seafood Salad!)

3   Blind Mice (See How They Run)

4   Quarts in a Gallon

24   Hours in a Day

1   Wheel on a Unicycle

9   Digits in a Zip Code

57   Heinz Varieties

11   Players on a Football Team

1000   Words that a Picture is Worth

29   Days in February in a Leap Year

64   Squares on a Checkerboard

40   Days and Nights of the Great Flood

4   Score and Seven Years Ago

Application

Help participants learn your jargon, abbreviations, and acronyms. Use this sheet as a fun exercise to show how we often abbreviate words to letters. Then hand out a similar sheet of your organization's abbreviations, jargon, and acronyms for participants to complete. Or weave some of your own content into this sheet.

See how many of these advertising jingles you can complete by filling in the blank(s).

1. "A spring, a spring, a marvelous thing—everyone knows it's _____."

2. "We love baseball, hot dogs, apple pie and _____."

3. "_____ tastes good, like a cigarette should."

4. "I'd like to buy the world a _____."

5. "Leggo my _____."

6. "Oh I wish I were an _____ _____ _____."

7. "Come see the softer side of _____."

8. "_____ time."

9. "The chicken's got that perfect _____ality."

10. "_____ country."

11. "_____ _____, don't leave home without it."

12. "Pardon me, would you have any _____ _____?"

13. "Nothing beats a great pair of _____."

14. "Fill it to the rim, with _____."

15. "_____ gets out what America gets into."

Communication: The Power of Repetition

Preparation

Make a handout from the master on the opposite page.

Solution

1. "A spring, a spring, a marvelous thing—everyone knows it's Slinky."
2. "We love baseball, hot dogs, apple pie and Chevrolet."
3. "Winston tastes good, like a cigarette should."
4. "I'd like to buy the world a Coke."
5. "Leggo my Eggo."
6. "Oh I wish I were an Oscar Mayer Weiner."
7. "Come see the softer side of Sears."
8. "Miller time."
9. "The chicken's got that perfect Wessonality."
10. "Marlboro country."
11. "American Express, don't leave home without it."
12. "Pardon me, would you have any Grey Poupon?"
13. "Nothing beats a great pair of Leggs."
14. "Fill it to the rim, with Brim."
15. "Tide gets out what America gets into."

Application

Advertisers know the power of repetition—we need to hear a message at least six times before it sticks in our memory. Use the power of repetition in your communication efforts. Use the power of repetition . . . (well, you get the idea!).

A first-grade teacher collected old, well-known proverbs. She gave each child in her class the first half of a proverb, and asked them to come up with the rest. Enjoy the students' responses, and then complete the proverb as you probably learned it.

1. As you make your bed so shall you . . .
   mess it up.   _____

2. Better to be safe than . . .
   to punch a 5th grader.   _____

3. Strike while the . . . bug is close.   _____

4. It's always darkest before the . . .
   daylight saving time.   _____

5. You can lead a horse to water but . . . how?   _____

6. Don't bite the hand that . . . looks dirty.   _____

7. A miss is as good as a . . . mister.   _____

8. You can't teach an old dog new . . . math.   _____

9. The pen is mightier than the . . . pigs.   _____

10. An idle mind is . . . the best way to relax.   _____

11. Where there's smoke, there's . . . pollution.   _____

12. A penny saved is . . . not much.   _____

13. Two's company, three's . . . the musketeers.   _____

14. Laugh and the world laughs with you, cry . . .
    and you have to blow your nose.   _____

15. Children should be seen and not . . .
    spanked or grounded.   _____

Communication: Avoid Making Assumptions

Preparation

Make a handout from the master on the opposite page.

Solution

1. As you make your bed, so shall you lie in it.
2. Better to be safe than sorry.
3. Strike while the iron is hot.
4. It's always darkest before the dawn.
5. You can lead a horse to water, but you can't make it drink.
6. Don't bite the hand that feeds you.
7. A miss is as good as a mile.
8. You can't teach an old dog new tricks.
9. The pen is mightier than the sword.
10. An idle mind is the devil's workshop.
11. Where there's smoke there's fire.
12. A penny saved is a penny earned.
13. Two's company, three's a crowd.
14. Laugh and the world laughs with you, cry and you cry alone.
15. Children should be seen and not heard.

Application

Don't assume people know what you are talking about. Other people's experiences are often different from ours. Spell it out. Communicate it simply without slang or proverbs.

Toothpick Trickery

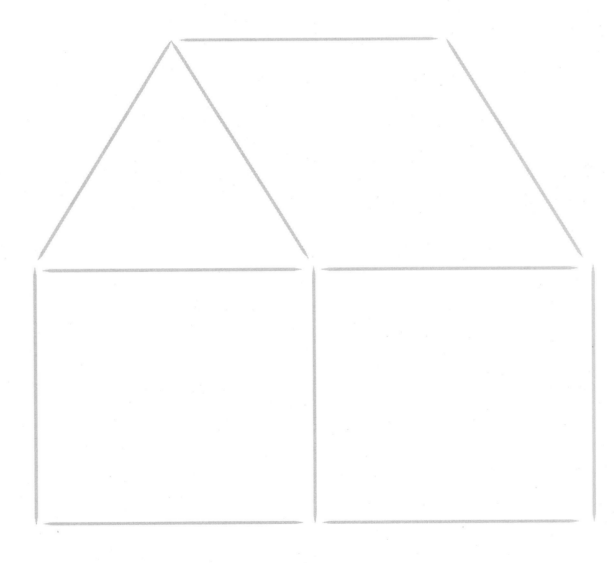

How did the trainer get the dog
to turn around by moving
only one toothpick?

The Trained Dog

Preparation

Duplicate the opposite page onto a transparency. Display the transparency on your overhead as a way of welcoming your participants into your training room.

Make sure that you also have 11 toothpicks for each participant so that all participants may experiment with the puzzle.

Solution

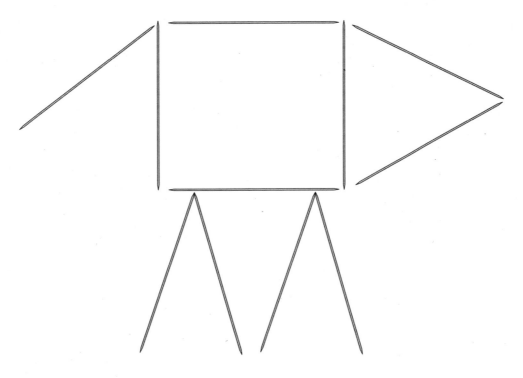

Application

The importance of little details is underscored—the movement of only one toothpick causes the dog to face the opposite direction.

Paying attention to details on the job is equally important!

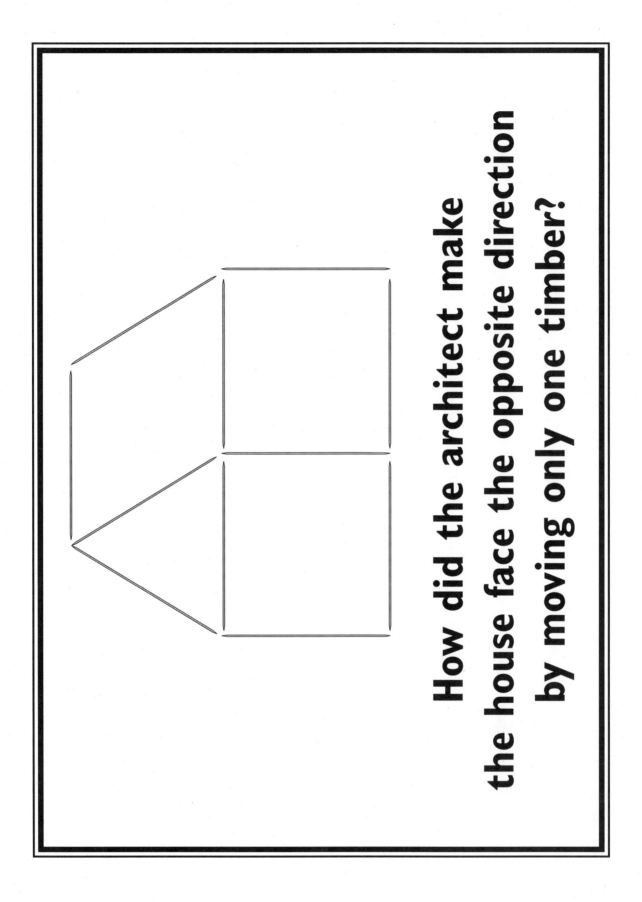

How did the architect make the house face the opposite direction by moving only one timber?

House Moving

Preparation

Duplicate the opposite page on a transparency and make sure that every person in your class has 11 toothpicks to work with in solving this problem.

Solution

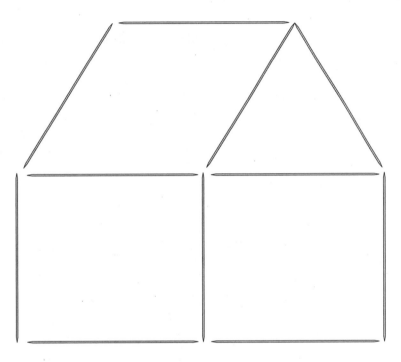

Application

The movement of one component in the house made a huge difference. What roles in a company would most people say are "small components" but really make a big difference when they are not working efficiently? Any other discussion about the small details making the big differences (for example, conflict, communication) would work equally well as themes for making a transition from this activity into your content.

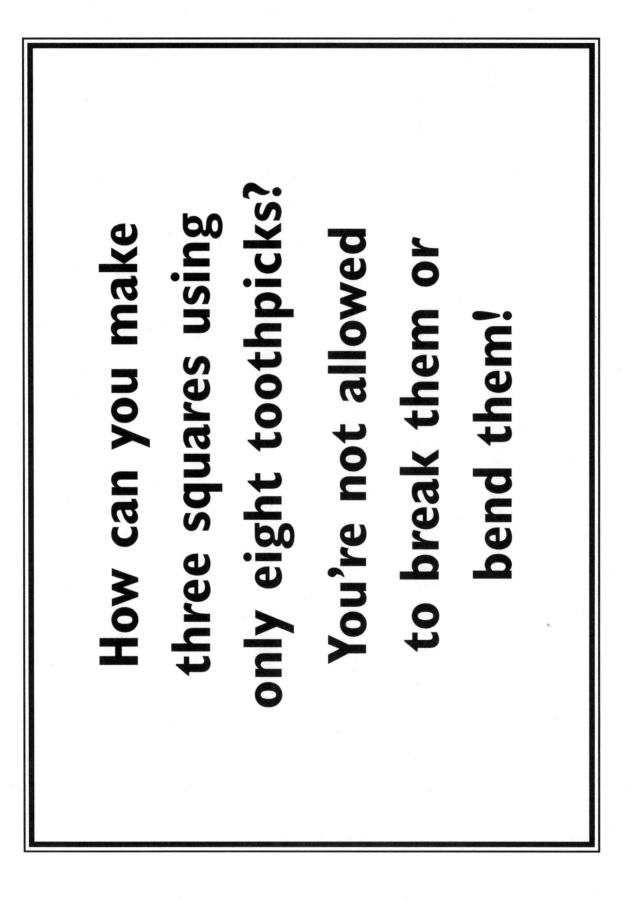

How can you you make three squares using only eight toothpicks? You're not allowed to break them or bend them!

Warming Up the Crowd! by Dave Arch and Rich Meiss.
Copyright © 2000 by Jossey-Bass/Pfeiffer and Creative Training Techniques Press, San Francisco, CA.

Toothpick Squares

Preparation

Duplicate the opposite page onto a transparency for use in introducing this activity. Make sure each person has eight toothpicks.

Solution

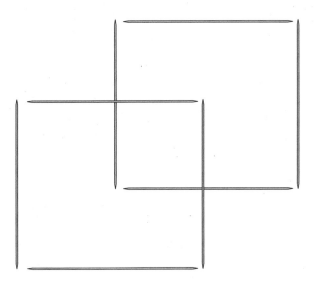

Application

Thinking outside the box (no pun intended) is necessary to solve this puzzle. What paradigm shifts had to occur in order to find a solution to this puzzle?

How is this similar to what must happen to be creative in the workplace?

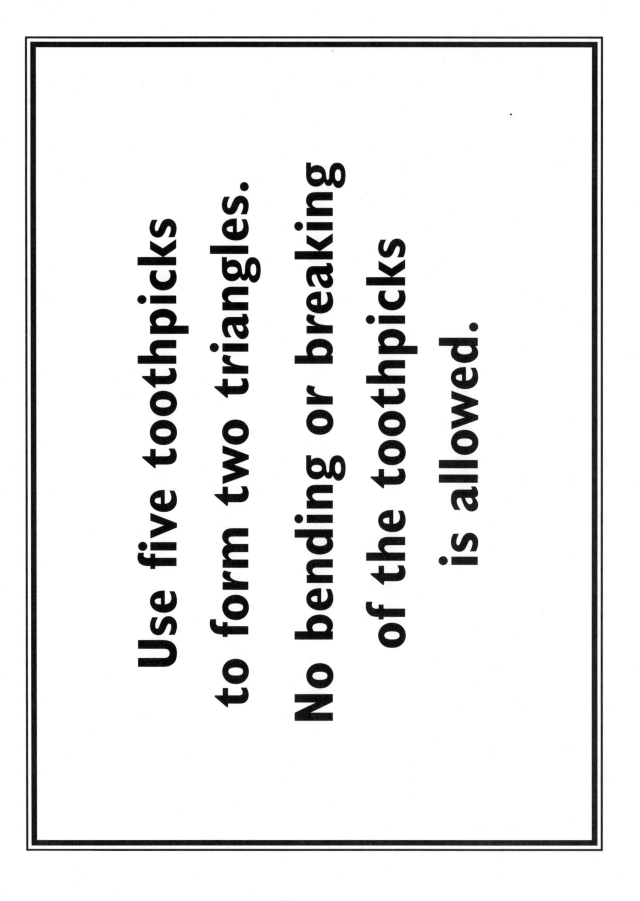

Use five toothpicks
to form two triangles.

No bending or breaking
of the toothpicks
is allowed.

Toothpick Triangles 1

Preparation

Duplicate the opposite page to use on your overhead as you introduce this pre-session activity. Have prizes available for the first team that successfully meets the challenge. Make sure that each person or team has access to five toothpicks so they may try to solve the puzzle.

Solution

Lay the toothpicks flat on the table and make one triangle of three toothpicks. Then share one side of the original triangle with the other two toothpicks.

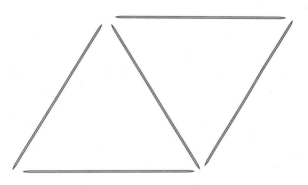

Application

This activity should come fairly easy, but you are really using this one as an introduction to the next activity.

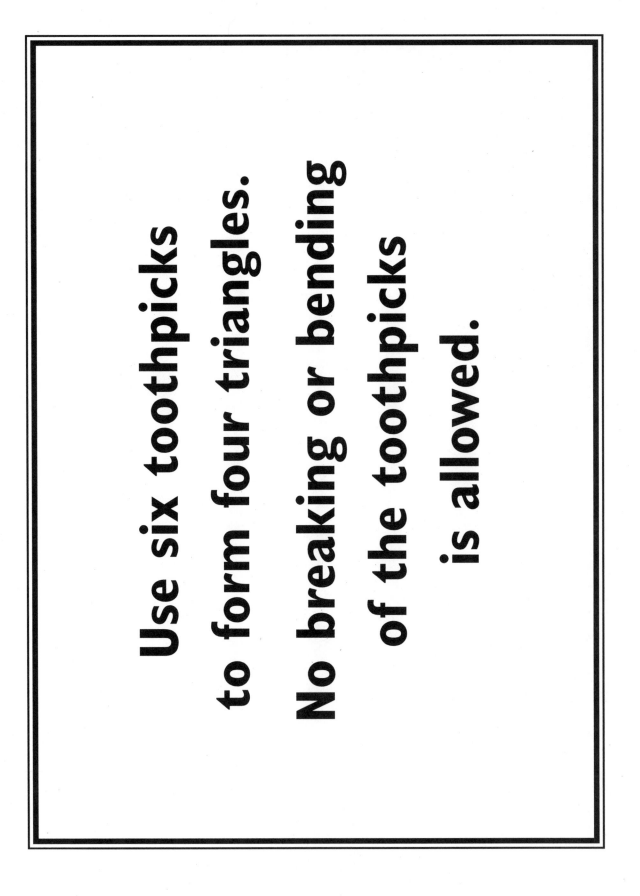

Use six toothpicks to form four triangles. No breaking or bending of the toothpicks is allowed.

Toothpick Triangles 2

Preparation

Duplicate the opposite page so that it can used as a transparency to introduce this challenging pre-session activity. Make sure that each person has access to six toothpicks as they attempt to solve the puzzle.

Solution

Think three-dimensional, with one triangle made with three toothpicks flat on the table, and then a three-toothpick tepee rising from the corners of this initial triangle.

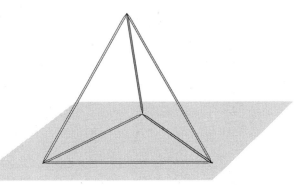

Application

Sometimes we make rules for ourselves that are totally unnecessary. Most participants will work over and over with the toothpicks flat on the table, never thinking of a three-dimensional figure. The elimination of the three-dimensional possibility happened only in our own minds.

What are some examples of rules from the workplace that we put upon ourselves, preventing us from being fully successful and perhaps as satisfied as we could be with our own jobs?

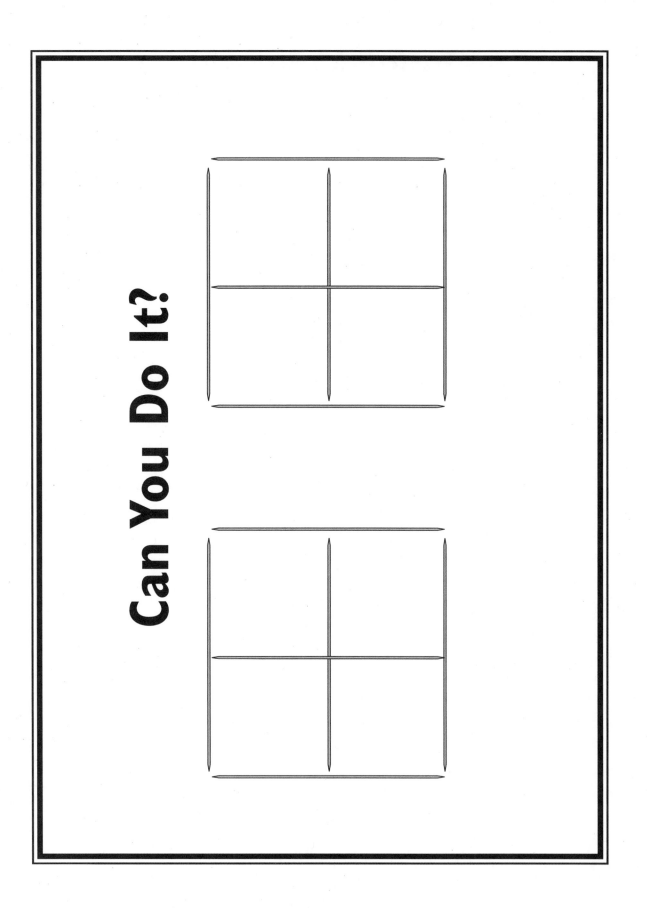

Can You Do It?

Toothpick Trickery

Preparation

Duplicate the opposite page onto a transparency so that participants have a pattern to use as they build their own design at the tables. Make sure each person or team has the 18 toothpicks needed to build the design. Each line in the diagram is comprised of one toothpick.

Presentation

You must *speak* this challenge to your participants: "Can you remove two of the toothpicks from the design and leave only ate?" They of course will hear the final "ate" as "eight" and attempt the impossible.

Solution

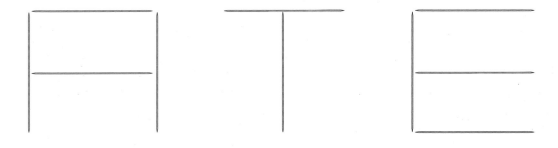

Application

This is a wonderful activity for demonstrating the role of paradigms (and context) in our communications. It also points to how often our assumptions about a statement (or a person) can lead us in a completely erroneous direction. Finally, it demonstrates graphically how spoken communication can be less precise than written communication.

Wuzzles®

Introduction to Wuzzles

Wuzzles are a perfect way to involve people at any point in a presentation: as a time-filler for people waiting for a session to start or for those who are back early from a break, and as an energizer to give people a mental break while keeping them focused.

Wuzzles (or rebuses) are word puzzles made up of combinations of words, letters, figures, or symbols that are positioned to create words, phrases, names, places, sayings, and such.

Some Wuzzles contain more than one concept and some can be created in several different ways. For example, here are four of the many versions of "Split up over nothing."

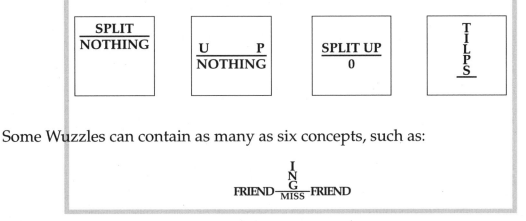

Some Wuzzles can contain as many as six concepts, such as:

FRIEND—MISS—FRIEND with ING above

(A little misunderstanding between a couple of close friends)

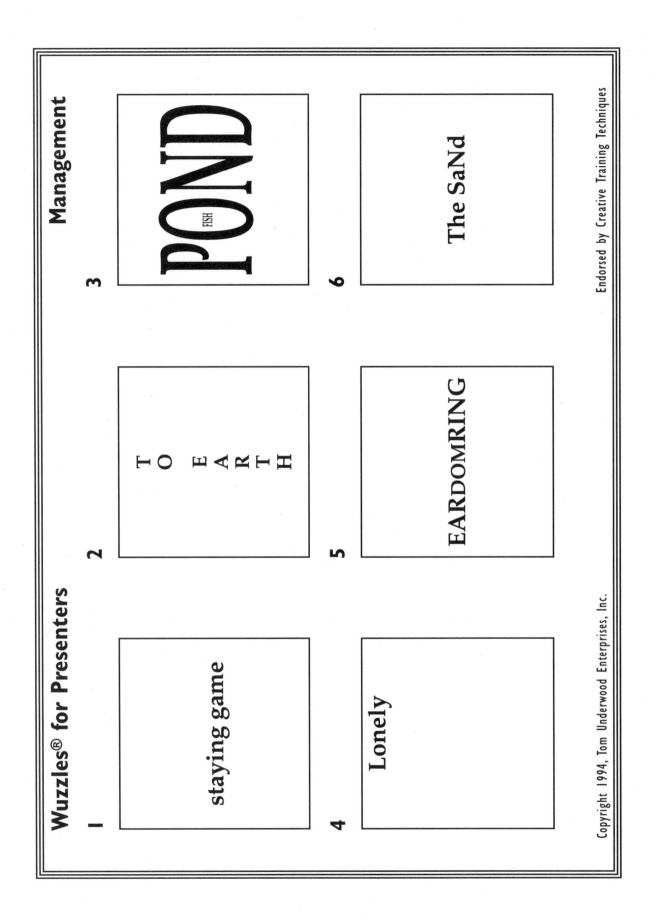

1. staying game

2.
   T
   O
   E
   A
   R
   T
   H

3. P_{FISH}OND

4. Lonely

5. EARDOMRING

6. The SaNd

Endorsed by Creative Training Techniques

Copyright 1994, Tom Underwood Enterprises, Inc.

Wuzzles for Presenters: Management

Preparation

Make a transparency of the master on the opposite page. As participants enter the room, ask them to solve the Wuzzles.

Solution

1. Staying ahead of the game
2. Down to earth
3. A small fish in a big pond
4. Lonely at the top
5. Domineering ("dom in earring")
6. Head in the sand

Application

In addition to waking up the brain and stimulating creativity, "wuzzles" can be used to send a message. An example of using them with a management group would be: "If our goal is 'staying ahead of the game,' then we should come 'down to earth' and recognize that there are no 'small fish in a big pond' around here. Even though it is sometimes 'lonely at the top,' we should avoid being 'domineering' and should not put our 'heads in the sand.'"

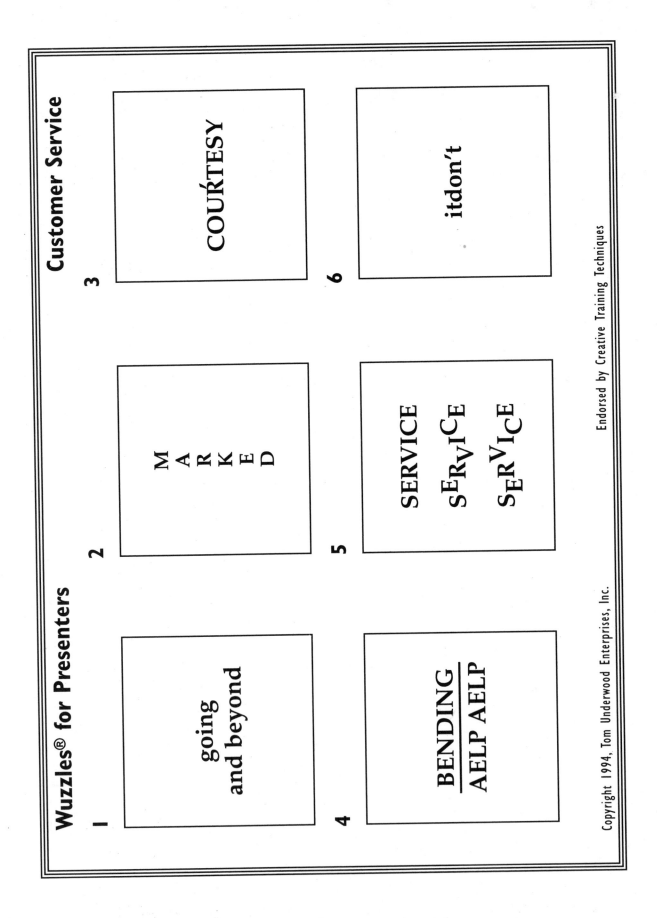

Wuzzles for Presenters: Customer Service

Preparation

Make a transparency of the master on the opposite page. As participants enter the room, ask them to first solve the Wuzzles and then connect them in a sentence that describes the customer service function in their organization.

Solution

1. Going above and beyond
2. Marked down
3. Common courtesy
4. Bending over backwards to please
5. Top-level service
6. Don't buy it

Application

"It is our goal here at the XYZ company to serve our customers by 'going above and beyond' so that they aren't always looking for our merchandise to be 'marked down.' As a 'common courtesy,' we will be 'bending over backwards to please' and giving 'top-level service'. We know that our customers 'don't buy it' if we don't offer them our best!"

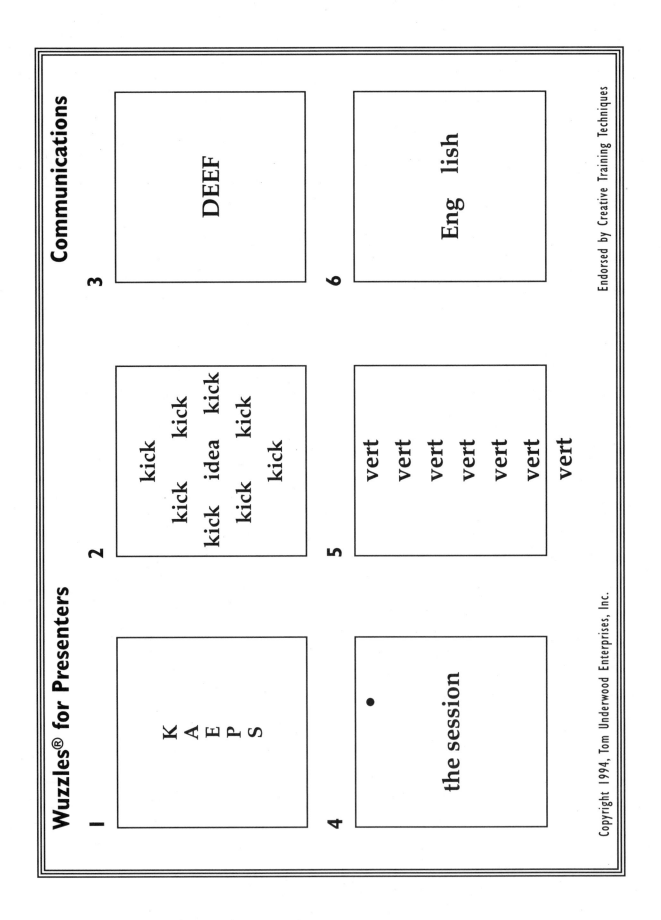

Wuzzles for Presenters:
Communications

Preparation

Make a transparency of the master on the opposite page. As participants enter the room, ask them to solve the Wuzzles.

Solution

1. Speak up
2. Kicks around an idea
3. Feedback
4. High point of the session
5. Extrovert
6. Broken English

Application

"In order to get the best results around here, it is important for you to 'speak up' when someone 'kicks around an idea.' Give them some 'feedback'; who knows, your thoughts may become the 'high point of the session.' So become an extrovert, whether you speak 'broken English' or perfect English."

Section 13

Read and Ponder

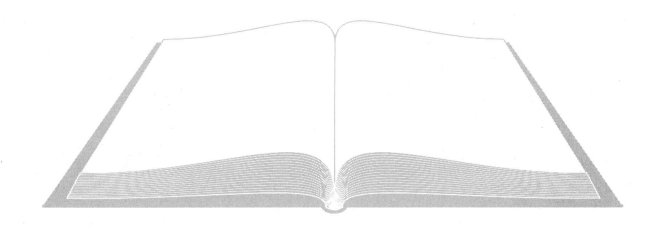

Read what some "experts" said in the past, and see if you can guess who said it. Are we caught in any similar kind of thinking today? What achievements would be possible if we focused on the task?

"This telephone has too many shortcomings to be seriously considered as a means of communication. The device is inherently of no value to us." _____

"Computers in the future may weigh no more than 1.5 tons."

_____

"Who the hell wants to hear actors talk?" _____

"I think there is maybe a world market for maybe five computers." _____

"Heavier-than-air flying machines are impossible." _____

_____

"Drill for oil? You mean drill into the ground to try and find oil? You're crazy!" _____

"There is no reason anyone would want a computer in their home." _____

"Everything that can be invented has been invented." _____

_____

"Who in their right mind would ever need more than 640K of RAM?" _____

"Stocks have reached what looks like a permanently high plateau." _____

"We don't like their sound, and guitar music is on the way out." _____

Motivation: Something to Ponder Today

Preparation

Make a copy of the opposite page and distribute to each participant.

Solution

"This telephone has too many shortcomings to be seriously considered as a means of communication. The device is inherently of no value to us."

Western Union internal memo, 1876

"Computers in the future may weigh no more than 1.5 tons."

Popular Mechanics *article, 1949*

"Who wants to hear actors talk?"   *H.M. Warner, Warner Brothers, 1927*

"I think there is a world market for maybe five computers."

Thomas Watson, chairman of IBM, 1943

"Heavier-than-air flying machines are impossible."

Lord Kelvin, president, Royal Society, 1895

"Drill for oil? You mean drill into the ground to try and find oil? You're crazy!"

Drillers whom Edwin L. Drake tried to enlist to help find oil, 1859

"There is no reason anyone would want a computer in their home."

Ken Olson, founder and president of Digital Equipment Corp., 1977

"Everything that can be invented has been invented."

Charles H. Duell, Commissioner, U.S. Office of Patents, 1899

"Who in their right mind would ever need more than 640K of RAM!?

Bill Gates, Microsoft Chairman, 1981

"Stocks have reached what looks like a permanently high plateau."

Irving Fisher, Professor of Economics at Yale, 1929

"We don't like their sound, and guitar music is on the way out."

Decca Recording Co., rejecting the Beatles, 1962

Application

Use this exercise to prepare for problem solving or brainstorming activities. Have participants read the statements and guess who said them. Then ask: What ideas seem improbable or impossible today, but may well be common practice in the future?

Sometimes the simplest philosophy, applied to our organization, can help us see things in a new way. Let's see how many insights we can come up with that relate one of these cowboy "funny's" to an application for our business or organization.

1. Don't squat with yer spurs on.

2. Never kick a fresh cow chip on a hot day.

3. Don't worry about bitin' off more than you can chew. Your mouth is probably a whole lot bigger'n you think.

4. If you get to thinkin' you're somebody of influence, try orderin' somebody else's dog around.

5. If you find yourself in a hole, the first thing to do is to stop diggin'.

6. It don't take a genius to spot a goat in a flock of sheep.

7. Never ask a barber if he thinks you need a haircut.

8. Good judgment comes from experience; experience comes from poor judgment.

9. Always drink upstream from the herd.

10. Never drop yer gun to hug a grizzly.

11. If you're ridin' ahead of the herd, look back now and then to make sure it's still there.

12. When you give a lesson in meanness to a critter or a person, don't be too surprised if they learn their lesson.

13. When you're throwin' your weight around, be ready to have it thrown around by somebody else.

14. Lettin' the cat outa the bag is a whole lot easier than puttin' it back.

15. Never miss a good chance to shut up.

Fun Warmups:
A Cowboy's Guide to Life

Preparation

Make a copy of the opposite page and distribute to each participant or table.

Solution

A few examples of insights are given below.

3. Are we limiting our accomplishments by thinking too small? Often we are capable of stretching farther and doing more than we would have ever imagined.

5. Stop doing those things that get poor results. Sometimes we do things just because "we've always done it that way"—even when those things no longer work.

7. To get honest opinions, remember to check with those who have no vested interest in the outcome. Objectivity can be a wonderful thing!

11. Remember to do some MBWA—management by walking around. Is our head in the clouds? Are we making sure our people know and embrace our vision?

15. We often learn more when we listen than when we talk.

Application

Sometimes our best thinking happens when we can laugh at life—and maybe at ourselves. Have meeting participants do some "out of the box" thinking; assign each person or a small group several cowboy phrases and have them come up with an insight about your business related to that phrase. You're sure to have some fun with this one! This activity is great for a meeting or training energizer!

Section 14

Personality Tests

Please circle the letter for only one answer for each of the questions below. Then you will be presented with the totally and completely nonscientific analysis of your answers.

You are walking through the woods when you come to a clearing. In the clearing there is a lake. Beside the lake there is a cup. You are thirsty.

1. **What do you do?**

   a. **Use the cup to take a drink from the lake?**

   b. **Leave the cup where it is?**

   c. **Examine the cup in order to decide what to do?**

2. **Then do you**

   a. **Put the cup back where it was?**

   b. **Leave it where it is?**

   c. **Take the cup away with you?**

The water in the lake looks inviting. You are warm.

3. **Do you**

   a. **Wash your face and hands in it?**

   b. **Go swimming in it?**

   c. **Stay out of it?**

You see a bear approaching you as you stand by the lake. He is walking slowly and evidently doesn't see you.

4. **Do you**

   a. **Run as fast as you can?**

   b. **Stand very still?**

   c. **Try to make friends with the bear?**

Personality Test 1

Preparation

Duplicate and distribute Personality Test 1 so that each person can complete the exercise before the class begins.

Solution

There is no correct or incorrect answer to any of the questions.

Presentation

At the beginning of your class, go through the interpretation of the questions (from page 166) with the group and you'll soon have them laughing and looking at each other's papers to see how other people answered the questions.

Application

This is a wonderful, lighthearted icebreaker because you get people interested in others at their table. It fills the room with energy when you ask for a show of hands and other participation at various points while reading the interpretations.

Please answer each of the questions below. Then you will be presented with the totally and completely nonscientific analysis of your answers.

1. Describe your dream garden.

   _____
   _____
   _____

2. Where is your house in relation to your garden?

   _____
   _____
   _____

3. What is the house like?

   _____
   _____
   _____

4. What is the key to your house like?

   _____
   _____
   _____

5. What would you do if you lost your key and wanted to get into your house?

   _____
   _____
   _____

6. You are standing alone holding something. What is it?

   _____
   _____
   _____

7. Near your garden is a house that belongs to someone else. It has a wall around it. There is a gate in the wall and a lock on the gate, but you have no key for this lock. You want to get in. What would you do?

   _____
   _____
   _____

Personality Test 2

Preparation

Distribute Personality Test 2 so that each person can complete the exercise before the class begins.

Solution

There is no correct or incorrect answer to any of the questions.

Presentation

At the beginning of your class, go through the interpretation of the questions (from page 167) with the group and you'll soon have them laughing and looking at each other's papers to see how other people answered the questions.

Application

This is a wonderful, lighthearted icebreaker because you get people interested in others at their table. It fills the room with energy when you ask for a show of hands and other participation at various points while reading the interpretations.

On the bottom of this page, please draw a picture of a pig.

Then you will be presented with the totally and completely nonscientific analysis of your drawing.

Personality Test 3

Preparation

Distribute Personality Test 3 so that each person can complete the exercise before the class begins.

Solution

There is no correct or incorrect way to draw the pig.

Presentation

At the beginning of your class, go through the interpretation of the drawing (from page 168) with the group and you'll soon have them laughing and looking at each other's papers to see how other people drew their pigs.

This is the most humorous of the personality tests. Don't be afraid to get participants really laughing. Laughing breaks down barriers and creates an openness that enhances teaching and learning.

Application

This is a wonderful, lighthearted icebreaker because you get people interested in others at their table; it helps fill the room with energy. This activity will also help establish the networking that is essential to create maximum retention of content by participants.

Please circle the letter that answers each of the questions below. Then you will be presented with the totally and completely nonscientific analysis of your answers.

1. You are walking to your lover's house. There are two roads to get there. One is a straight path to take you there quickly, but it is very plain and boring. The other is significantly longer but is full of wonderful sights and interesting things. Which one do you take?

    a. The short, boring one?

    b. The long, interesting one?

2. Along the way you see two rose bushes. One is full of red roses, the other full of white. You decide to pick 20 roses for your lover. What number of white and red roses do you pick? You can pick all one color or mix the colors.

    a. Red roses _____

    b. White roses _____

(The numbers in the two blanks must total twenty roses.)

3. You finally reach the house. A family member answers the door. Do you

    a. Ask the person to go and get your lover?

    b. Go and get your lover yourself?

4. You go to your lover's room, but nobody is there. You decide to leave the roses. Do you

    a. Leave the roses by the window?

    b. Leave the roses on the bed?

5. Later, when it's time for bed, you and your lover go to sleep in separate rooms. In the morning you go to check on your lover. When you arrive

    a. Your lover is awake already.

    b. Your lover is still asleep.

6. Now it's time to go back home. Do you

    a. Take the short, boring road?

    b. Take the long, interesting road?

Personality Test 4

Preparation

Distribute Personality Test 4 so that each person can complete the exercise before the class begins.

Solution

There is no correct or incorrect answer to any of the questions.

Presentation

At the beginning of your class, go through the interpretation of the questions (from page 169) with the group, and you'll soon have them laughing and looking at each other's papers to see how other people answered the questions.

Application

This is a wonderful, lighthearted icebreaker to get people interested in others at their table and to fill the room with energy.

Personality Test 1 Interpretation

Question 1 tests your attitude toward other people.

  a. You are outgoing, friendly, and sometimes not as cautious as you might be.

  b. You wait for other people to approach you, offering your friendship to only a few.

  c. Your attitude toward others is based on a balanced approach of using caution mixed with common sense.

Question 2 is a test of your attitude toward your friends.

  a. Your friendships are often casual, with you making few demands on your friends.

  b. You are easily offended and don't open up easily to even your closest friends.

  c. You are possessive of your friends even to the point of being demanding and jealous.

Question 3 is a test of your attitude toward new experiences.

  a. You test out new activities before committing yourself to them.

  b. You rush into new things and leave them just as quickly.

  c. You are reluctant to participate in new activities.

Question 4 is a test of your attitude toward life.

  a. You run away from it.

  b. You wait to see what's going to happen before taking action.

  c. You go out to meet it, even sometimes without thinking.

Personality Test 2 Interpretation

Question 1   Your description of your secret garden is the way you want everyone to think of you.

Questions 2 and 3   The location and description of your house are a description of yourself in relation to the rest of the world.

Question 4   The key is a description of your friendships in relation to their complexity or simplicity.

Question 5   This describes what you do when something goes wrong in a relationship.

Question 6   Whatever you choose to describe represents the artistic and imaginative sides of your personality.

Question 7   The action you take reveals what you do when faced with an obstacle.

Personality Test 3 Interpretation

If the pig is drawn:

- toward the top of the paper, you are positive and optimistic.
- toward the middle of the paper, you are a realist.
- toward the bottom of the paper, you are negative and pessimistic.

If the pig:

- faces left, you believe in tradition.
- faces right, you are innovative and active.
- faces forward (looking at you), you are direct and forthright.
- faces the rear, seek counseling immediately. (That's a joke.)

If the pig is drawn with:

- many details, you are analytical.
- few details, you are a risk taker and sometimes commit before analyzing an entire situation.
- fewer than four legs showing, you are living in a time of major personal change.
- four legs showing, you are secure and sometimes stubborn.
- more than four legs showing, seek professional help. (Another joke.)

The size of the ears indicates how good a listener you are—the bigger the better.

The length of the tail indicates the quality of your love life. The longer the tail, the more fulfilling your love life.

Did you even draw a tail?

Personality Test 4 Interpretation

Personality Test 4 analyzes your approach toward relationships.

Question 1   The road represents your attitude toward falling in love. If you take the short road, you fall in love quickly and easily. If you take the long road, you take your time and do not fall in love as easily.

Question 2   The number of red roses represents how much you give in a relationship, while the number of white represents what you expect in return. For example, if you chose 18 red and 2 white, you give 90 percent and expect 10 percent in return.

Question 3   This question represents your attitude toward handling relationship problems. If you asked the family member to get your lover, then you like to avoid problems and hope that they will solve themselves. If you went to get your lover, then you are a more direct person and like to work out problems immediately.

Question 4   The placement of roses determines how much you like to see your lover. Placing them on the bed means you like to see your lover a lot. Placing them by the window means that you are all right with not seeing your lover as often.

Question 5   This is representative of your attitude toward your lover's personality. If you find your lover asleep, you appreciate your lover for the way he or she is. If you find your lover awake, you expect your lover to change for you.

Question 6   The road to home tells how long you stay in love with someone. If you chose the short road, it means that you fall out of love more easily than someone who chose the long road.

Remember: this is an unscientific test. Any result that coincides with your actual approach to relationships is purely coincidental.

More great resources from Jossey-Bass/Pfeiffer!

End your sessions with a BANG!

Lynn Solem & Bob Pike
50 Creative Training Closers

They'll forget you as soon as you walk out the door—unless you make your training memorable. This essential resource is your way to make your mark. Fifty ways to close your training sessions and presentations so they won't forget you—or your training.

Many trainers start training sessions memorably with a rousing icebreaker, or with a spirited overview of what's to follow. But you're probably letting the ends slip through your fingers. Some trainers conclude training sessions by looking at their watches and saying, "Oh, time's up! Goodbye!" By trailing off with a whisper, you're missing an opportunity to reinforce your training. You're helping your participants to forget everything you've taught them. Stop this brain drain by ending with a bang! This invaluable book is packed with practical closers.

You get activities great for:

- *Reviewing* material
- *Celebrating* success
- *Motivating* participants . . . and more!

Solem and Pike show you all the essentials, and preparation is quick and easy. So little time to invest for such a HUGE payoff! This book is training dynamite—make it your secret weapon today.

paperback / 96 pages

50 Creative Training Closers
Item #F439

Bob Pike & Dave Arch
Dealing with Difficult Participants

127 Practical Strategies for Minimizing Resistance and Maximizing Results in Your Presentations

Everyone knows them . . . but almost no one knows how to deal with them. Difficult participants. The "latecomer." The "know-it-all." The "confused." What do you do? Train-the-trainer master Bob Pike and magician/trainer Dave Arch have the answers.

Learn to deal with types such as:

- The Preoccupied
- The Socializer
- The Introvert
- The Bored
- The Domineering
- The Unqualified
- The Skeptic
- The Sleeper . . . and others!

Don't let difficult participants get the best of you. You can't afford not to pick up this engaging book. Maximize the learning potential in all your presentations with *Dealing With Difficult Participants*!

paperback / 150 pages

Dealing with Difficult Participants
Item #F244

To order, please contact your local bookstore, call us toll-free at 1-800-274-4434, or visit us on the Web at www.pfeiffer.com.

13 Questions to Ask *Before* You Bring Anyone In-House

An in-house program is an investment. You want to ensure high return. Here are 13 questions to ask before you ask anyone to train your trainers (or train anyone else!).

1. What kind of measurable results have other clients had from your training?
2. How much experience does this company have in training trainers?
3. Is this 100 percent of what the company does or just part of what it does?
4. How experienced are the trainers who will work with our people?
5. How experienced are your trainers in maximizing training transfer to the job?
6. Is the program tailored to my needs, or is it the same content as the public program?
7. Why is an in-house program to our advantage?
8. Is team-building a by-product of the seminar?
9. Is there immediate application of new skills during the training session?
10. What kinds of resource and reference materials do we get?
11. What type of pre-course preparation or post-course follow-up do you do?
12. How are our participants recognized for their achievements?
13. Will you teach my trainers how to get participant buy-in, even from the difficult participant?

Advantages of a Customized, In-House Program with Creative Training Techniques™ International, Inc.

Customized in-house programs provide your organization with training tailored to your specific needs. Our unique participant-centered teaching style is a revolutionary new training approach that is far more effective than traditional lecture-based training. This training approach has been adapted by a wide range of industries including healthcare, finance, communications, government, and non-profit agencies. Our clients include American Express, AT&T, Hewlett-Packard, 3M, U.S. Healthcare, and Tonka Corporation. We are eager to learn about your training needs and discuss how we can provide solutions. Please give us a call so we can help your company create a more vital and effective workforce.

Creative Training Techniques
International, Inc.

1–800–383–9210
www.cttbobpike.com

Creative Training Techniques International, Inc. • 7620 W. 78th St., Mpls., MN 55439 • 612-829-1954 • Fax 612-829-0260

Bob Pike's
Creative Training Techniques™
Train-the-Trainer Conference

*The only conference dedicated exclusively
to the participant-centered approach to training*

- Learn about the revolutionary, participant-centered training approach—the breakthrough alternative to lecture-based training
- See the nation's leading training consultants model their very best participant-centered activities
- Experience the power of participant-centered techniques to dramatically increase retention
- Learn about innovative training transfer techniques adopted by leading Fortune 500 companies
- Discover powerful management strategies that clearly demonstrate the business results for your training programs

Just a few of the companies who have sent groups (not just individuals) to the Conference

**American Express • AT&T • Caterpillar • First Bank
Southern Nuclear Operating Company • State Farm • United HealthCare • US West**

Rave Reviews!

"I refer to my conference workbook all the time. I've shared the techniques with my trainers, and my own evaluations have improved. Our needs analysis now produces actionable input. My comfort level with our line managers has increased—at my first meeting with them where I used what I learned at the conference, they applauded. Now that's positive feedback!"

Gretchen Gospodarek, Training Manager, **TCF Bank Wisconsin**

"For any trainer who wants to move beyond lecture-based training, I recommend Bob Pike's participant-centered seminars and in-house consultants."

Ken Blanchard, Co-Author of *The One-Minute Manager*

"Bob Pike is creating a new standard in the industry by which all other programs will soon be measured."

Elliott Masie, President, **The MASIE Center**

Visit our Web site: www.cttbobpike.com to learn more about the Conference,
Creative Training Techniques International, Inc. or the Participant-Centered Training approach.

Creative Training Techniques
International, Inc.

1-800-383-9210
www.cttbobpike.com

Creative Training Techniques International, Inc. • 7620 W. 78th St., Mpls., MN 55439 • 612-829-1954 • Fax 612-829-0260